2ND MUFFY VANDI

IDENTIFICATION & PRICE

CW01550038

by Ann Gehlbach

Published by Hobby House Press
Grantsville, Maryland 21536
www.hobbyhouse.com

Photography by North American Bear Company
See pages: Front Cover, 1, 4-6, 9, 13, 15, 18-23, 26, 29, 33, 35, 37-38, 40-41, 43, 46, 48 (top), 49 (bottom), 51 (top), 52, 54 (top), 55 (top), 58 (top left & bottom), 60 (bottom), 62, 64 (top), 65, 66, 71, 73 (top), 75, 79, 80-89, 91-125, Back Cover.
Photography by Ric Miracle
See pages: 3, 10-12, 14, 16-17, 24-25, 27-28, 30-32, 34, 36, 39, 42, 44-45, 47, 48 (bottom), 49 (top), 50, 51 (bottom), 53, 54 (bottom), 55 (bottom), 56-57, 58 (top right), 59, 60 (top), 61, 63, 64 (bottom), 67-70, 72, 73 (bottom), 74, 76-78, 90, 126-134.

Front Cover: Muffy and Hoppy **Millenium Collection, From Dusk to Dawn.** *See page 113 for more information.*
Title Page: Muffy and Hoppy **Sleep Over Collection.** *See page 110 for more information.*
Back Cover: Cornelius, Fuzzy, Alice, Fluffy, Muffy and Hoppy **Garden Party.** *See page 116 for more information.*

BIOGRAPHY:

Ann Gehlbach lives in Sarasota, Florida with her husband Don. They have been collecting bears for over thirteen years. Ann was bitten by the "Muffy Bug" about eleven years ago, when she purchased her first Muffy for her daughter's Christmas present. Eight years ago their bear collection outgrew their home and Ann and Don opened Village Bears & Collectibles in Sarasota, Florida. Frustrated at being unable to answer their customers' many questions about Muffy, Ann decided to compile a VanderBear history as a reference guide for herself. That little project soon got out of hand and after three years of research, that original three page history had grown into a book! Through their web site <http://www.villagebears.com>, Ann has met hundreds of Muffy collectors from all over the world. Many have become cherished friends and each one helped to write this guide to Muffy's life. Through this experience, Ann has found that Muffy fanatics all have two things in common......a sense of humor and a devotion to Muffy. After all, who could not love a little seven inch bear who loves dressing up and has so much fun!

ACKNOWLEDGMENT

I would like to thank North American Bear Company and the Muffy collectors around the world for their help and support during the research of this second edition of the Muffy Identification Guide.

Additional copies of this book may be purchased at $22.95 (plus postage and handling) from
Hobby House Press, Inc.
1 Corporate Drive
Grantsville, Maryland 21536
www.hobbyhouse.com
1-800-554-1447
or from your favorite bookstore or dealer.

TABLE OF CONTENTS

Muffy
Muffy
Muffy
Muffy
Muffy
Muffy
Muffy
Muffy
Muffy
Muffy
Muffy
Muffy
Muffy
Muffy
Muffy
Muffy

How many Muffys do you see?

Life is One

A bouncing little bundle of fuzz was delivered to VanderBear Manor in 1984. Wearing an eyelet trimmed christening gown, Muffy was welcomed as the littlest member of the VanderBear Family, and nothing's been the same since. She keeps the whole family on the go, and that's just the way they like it. The family includes poppa Cornelius, an inventor and philosopher-at-large; kind and cultured momma Alice; and brother and sister Fuzzy and Fluffy (they're twins, but to tell you the truth, they're nothing alike).

Where do the VanderBears live? Well, let's just say you can look for them in the State of Exaggeration. If you happen to drop in, they'll probably declare a holiday and throw you a party. They celebrate any and all holidays and occasions (including a few they've made up). The VanderBears love wearing the costumes and learning the customs of all the places they visit around the world.

Muffy has many friends, pets, and pals whom she has made during her young lifetime…like Oatsie, the one-trick pony; Lulu, a Scottish

Big Dress Up

MacFluff (a rather rare breed of pup); and Purrlie, the calico kitten. But none can compare to her best friend and bosom bunny, the wild and glamorous Hoppy VanderHare, who accompanies the VanderBears on many of their adventures.

As you turn these pages, you will see that Muffy has an outfit for almost any occasion, because she believes that the best way to have an adventure is to dress up for it. After all, as Muffy always says…

"life is one big dress-up."

This excerpt appears in the front of the Muffy Vanderbear® 2000 Spring Collection Catalog.
Used with permission.

HOW TO USE THIS GUIDE

Author Ann Gehlbach has researched each and every Muffy release to aid you in identification purposes. Arranged chronologically by year of release, the collection name. Full descriptions of members costumes, and retirement dates are provided. Variations are categorized and an accompanying photograph captures the whimsical love of Muffy and her family. Keep in mind, that even though this guide has involved years of research and the help of many collectors, there will always be a different variation or another fact that is yet to be discovered. Just because it isn't listed, doesn't mean that it doesn't exist! Some collectors have also noticed differences in some tags that are sewn into Muffy's outfits, but since many of the early outfits did not have tags, documentation proved impossible.

Besides descriptions and variations, other helpful information is included. Hangtags for each Muffy are either described or featured in the photograph. Another common question that collectors ask – "How do I tell if a bear is factory dressed?" is answered in a special "The Bare Facts" section which includes exact wording of sewn-in tags of older Muffys and a few examples of outfits that came factory dressed on that particular Muffy. If that's not enough, test your Muffy knowledge in "More Muffy Trivia."

Enjoy this peek into Muffy's life!

A QUICK GUIDE TO MUFFY AND HER FAMILY

1983
Classic Velvet Family (1983-1988)
Cornelius • Alice • Fluffy • Fuzzy

1984
Muffy Christening (1984-)

1985
Red Flannel Holiday Collection (1985-1985)
Cornelius • Alice • Fluffy • Fuzzy • Muffy

1986
Muffy Valentine I (1986-1989)
Cruisewear Collection (1986-1991)
Cornelius • Alice • Fluffy • Fuzzy • Muffy
Muffy Witch (1986-1988)
Taffeta Holiday Collection (1986-1986)
Cornelius • Alice • Fluffy • Fuzzy • Muffy

1987
A Day In The Country (1987-1991)
Cornelius • Alice • Fluffy • Fuzzy • Muffy
Nutcracker Holiday Collection (1987-1987)
Cornelius • Alice • Fluffy • Fuzzy • Muffy

1988
Out of It In Africa (1988-1992)
Cornelius • Alice • Fluffy • Fuzzy • Muffy
Muffy Black Cat (1988-1995)
Furrier and Ives, The Skating Party (1988-1988)
Cornelius • Alice • Fluffy • Fuzzy • Muffy

1989
Muffy Valentine II (1989-1991)
Muffy Bunny (1989-)
High Tea Collection (1989-1992)
Cornelius • Alice • Fluffy • Fuzzy • Muffy
Muffy Pilgrim (1989-)
Tree Trimming Holiday Collection (1989-1989)
Cornelius • Alice • Fluffy • Fuzzy • Muffy • Scottie
Muffy Angel (1989-1989)

1990
Muffy Valentine III (1990-1994)
Muffy St. Patrick's Day (1990-1998)
Muffy Chick (1990-1994)
Muffy At The Beach (1990-1998)
Gibearny Collection (1990-1993)
Cornelius • Alice • Fluffy • Fuzzy • Muffy
Rembearances, (1990-1991) Cornelius • Alice
Back to School (1990-1993) Muffy • Hoppy
Sweet Dreams Collection (1990-1993)
Cornelius • Alice • Fluffy • Fuzzy • Muffy
Musical Soiree Collection (1990-1992)
Cornelius • Alice • Fluffy • Fuzzy • Muffy
Muffy, Little Fir Tree (1990-1990)

1991
Mommy & Me Collection (1991-1994) Alice • Muffy
Easter Fantasy (1991-1996) Muffy • Hoppy
The Wild West Collection (1991-1994)
Cornelius • Alice • Fluffy • Fuzzy • Muffy • Oatsie
Paw de Deux (1991-2001) Muffy • Hoppy
The Fortune Tellers (1991-2000) Muffy • Hoppy
The Ballet Recital (1991-1994) Muffy • Hoppy
Muffy SnowBear (1991-1991)
Bal Masque Collection (1991-1993) Cornelius • Alice •
Fluffy • Fuzzy • Muffy • Hoppy • Oatsie
Muffy Butterfly LE 10,000 (1991-1993)
1st Club Edition
Underthings (1991-1999) Muffy • Hoppy

1992
Down on the Farm (1992-1999)
Muffy • Patti • Rudy • Mary • Lucy • Webster
Dutch Treat (1992-1995) Muffy • Hoppy
Cherry Pie Collection (1992-1998) Cornelius • Muffy
Picnic Collection (1992- 1996)
Cornelius • Alice • Fluffy • Fuzzy • Muffy
Yankee Doodle (1992-1994) Muffy • Hoppy
Rainy Day (1992-1999) Muffy • Hoppy
Alpine Holiday Collection (1992-1994) Cornelius •
Alice • Fluffy • Fuzzy • Muffy • Hoppy • Oatsie
Muffy GingerBear (1992-1992)

1993
Kyoto Blossoms (1993-1996) Muffy • Hoppy
Flower Festival (1993-1995) Muffy • Hoppy • Oatsie •
Patti • Rudy • Mary • Lucy • Webster •
Bud and Rose, not retired
VdBeekeeping Collection (1993-1997)
Cornelius • Alice • Fluffy • Fuzzy • Muffy • Hoppy
The Sewing Lesson (1993-2000)
Fluffy • Muffy • Hoppy
The Equestrienne Collection (1993-1996)
Muffy • Hoppy • Oatsie
The Grand Tour, Travels with Muffy (1993-)
Highland Fling Holiday Collection (1993-1995)
Alice • Cornelius • Fluffy • Fuzzy • Muffy • Hoppy •
Lulu
Muffy Snowflake (1993-1993)
Muffy Rose LE 10,000 (1993-1994) 2nd Club Edition

1994
Egg Painting, Walking In Eggshells (1994-1994)
Muffy • Hoppy
The Queen of Hearts and Bunny Knave (1994-1998)
Muffy • Hoppy
The Boudoir Collection, Muffy (1994-1999)
Tricky Treat Trio (1994-1997) Muffy • Hoppy • Oatsie
Bathtime Collection, Splish Splash (1994-1998)
Muffy • Hoppy
Muffy of the North (1994-1994)

A QUICK GUIDE TO MUFFY AND HER FAMILY

North Pole Collection (1994-1996) Cornelius • Alice •
Fluffy • Fuzzy • Muffy • Hoppy • Lulu
Muffy 10th Anniversary (1994-1994)
Club House Collection (1994-1999)
Fuzzy • Muffy • Hoppy

1995
Pajama Game (1995-1999)
Fluffy • Fuzzy • Muffy • Hoppy
The Mozart Collection (1995-2000) Muffy • Hoppy
Princess and The Pea LE 15,000 (1995-1997) 3rd Club
All Paws On Deck (1995-1999) Cornelius • Alice
Fluffy • Fuzzy • Muffy • Hoppy • Lulu
Checkmates (1995-1999) Muffy • Hoppy
Czarina Muffina (1995-1997)
Sleddin' and Skidaddlin' (1995-2001)
Muffy • Hoppy • Lulu
Muffy Mouse (1995-1995)
New England Country Christmas (1995-1997) Alice •
Cornelius • Fluffy • Fuzzy • Muffy • Hoppy • Lulu

1996
Paint The Town Red LE 4500 (1996-1996)
Cornelius • Alice
Muffy Hearts and Flowers (1996-)
Hoppy Cocoa Bunny (1996-)
Spring Bonnets (1996-1997) Muffy • Hoppy • Lulu
The Reading Collection (1996-2000)
Muffy • Purrlie, not retired
Take A Hike Collection (1996-2000)
Cornelius • Alice • Fluffy • Fuzzy • Muffy • Hoppy
Muffy Pierrot LE 20,000 (1996-1996)
Happy Birthday To You! (1996-2000)
Muffy • Hoppy • Lulu • Oatsie
Cheerleading (1996-2000) Muffy • Hoppy • Lulu
Muffy The Red-Nosed ReinBear (1996-1996)
A Christmas Carol Bearly In Tune (1996-1998)
Cornelius • Alice • Fluffy • Fuzzy • Muffy • Hoppy •
Lulu • Oatsie

1997
Hoppy Messenger of Love (1997-)
A Salad Ballad Collection (1997-1999)
Fluffy • Muffy • Hoppy • Lulu • Purrlie
Square Dancing (1997-) Muffy • Hoppy • Lulu • Patti
the Cow
Mercy Me Hospital (1997-2001) Muffy • Hoppy • Lulu
Hoppus Poke-Us, Hoppy, LE 10,000 (1997-1997)
Puttering Around LE 3,500 (1997-1997)
Cornelius • Alice
Lemonade Stand (1997-) Muffy • Hoppy • Purrlie
Foolish Ghoulish, Scared Stiff (1997-)
Muffy • Hoppy • Lulu • Purrlie
Paris Bistrot (1997-) Muffy • Hoppy • Lulu
Portrait In Black & White Holiday Collection (1997-)
Cornelius • Alice • Fluffy • Fuzzy •
Muffy • Hoppy • Lulu • Purrlie

Muffy Tree Topper (1997-)
Muffy Candy C'angel (1997-1997)
The Little MerBear LE 15,000 (1997-1999) 4th Club
Muffy Peddler Doll LE 5,000 (1997-1997)

1998
Sweets For The Sweet (1998-2000)
Muffy • Hoppy • Lulu • Rudy
Muffy Spring Chickens (1998-)
Blue Pagoda (1998-) Muffy • Hoppy • Lulu • Purrlie
Abearicana (1998-) Muffy • Hoppy • Oatsie
Picking Posies (1998-) Alice • Muffy • Lulu
Signature Collection (1998-) Muffy • Hoppy
Muffy Little BearPeep LE 15,000 (1998-1998)
Hoppy PocaHoppy (1998-)
Muffy Plum Fairy (1998-1998)
Grand VanderBall Collection (1998-) Cornelius •
Alice • Fluffy • Fuzzy • Muffy • Hoppy • Lulu • Purrlie
Play Date Collection (1998-) Muffy • Hoppy

1999
Sleep Over Collection (1999-) Muffy • Hoppy
Jam Session Collection (1999-) Muffy • Hoppy
Splash Party (1999-) Muffy • Hoppy
Hit The Road (1999-) Muffy • Hoppy • Lulu • Purrlie
The Garden Party Collection (1999-)
Cornelius • Alice • Fluffy • Fuzzy • Muffy • Hoppy
Miss Muffy Belle (1999-1999)
Muffy Squir'lfriend (1999-)
Muffy Polar Bear (1999–1999)
Adirondack Collection, All Spruced Up (1999-)
Cornelius • Alice • Fluffy • Fuzzy • Muffy • Hoppy
Lulu • Purrlie • Bruce
Millennium Collection LE 2,000 (1999-1999)
Muffy • Hoppy
Little Miss Muffy (1999-2000) Fourth Club Edition

2000
Fabeargë Egg Collection (2000-) Muffy • Hoppy
All Over In Clover: The Shamrock Collection (2000-)
Picnic In Provence Collection (2000-)
Muffy • Hoppy • Lulu • Purrlie • Oatsie
Artistes At Work (2000-) Muffy • Hoppy
Daisy Petals (2000-)
Muffy Ahead of Her Time (2000-2000)
Cirque de la Lune Collection (2000-)
Muffy • Hoppy • Lulu • Purrlie • Oatsie
A Bushel Of Fun, Apple Antics (2000-)
Muffy • Hoppy
Deck the Halls With Bows & Dollies (2000-)
Muffy • Hoppy • Lulu • Purrlie
Muffy Winter Princess (2000-2000)
Muffy A Spot of Tea (2000-2001) Sixth Club Edition

VanderBear Family® History

**Classic Velvet
Family**, 1983
Left to right:
Fuzzy, Alice
(Muffy),
Cornelius, Fluffy.

The Classic Velvet Collection

Introduced in North American's 1983 catalog as "The Classic Teddy Bear Family (Jointed)". Most were tush tag bears, available both dressed and undressed.

20" Cornelius: black velvet trousers, suspenders, white shirt, bow tie

18" Alice: black velvet drop-waist dress with lace cuffs, lace neck inset, white ribbon sash

12" Fluffy: black velvet smock dress with white lace collar, white headbow

12" Fuzzy: black velvet knickers with two buttons, white shirt, black ribbon bow tie

✳Variation: Alice's first dress had pearl buttons in back, the second version had snaps.

Muffy Christening

First appeared in North American's 1994 Supplement Catalog as "The New Arrival". At 7" tall in white christening gown and cap with ribbon ties, this first Muffy was a tush tag bear and was also available without clothing.

✳*Variations (from left to right):*

Christening I: gown sewn shut on tush tag bear (a few issued with sewn gowns on tiny loop bear), retired

Christening II: gown with 2 snaps in back, some tush tag bears and some tiny loop bears, retired

Christening III: gown fastened with 1 button and 1 snap in back, retired

Christening IV: gown fastened with pink ribbon ties in back, still current

The fabric, eyelet trim, flowers, and ribbons also vary, but the different fastenings on the back of the gown are the easiest way to tell which version you have.

Hangtag Note
The Christening hangtag is the same hangtag that is used on the bare Muffy. The first was a large single hangtag. Later, a small folded hangtag was used.
For the first few years most hangtags came with white string. After that, gold elastic cord was the most common.

The Red Flannel Collection

VanderBear Family Holiday Limited Edition, limited to one year of production, tush tag bears dressed for a cozy Christmas Eve supper.

Cornelius: red flannel robe with a black cord tie, red flannel pajama bottoms, green paisley ascot

Alice: red flannel nightgown, round yoke with flannel ruffle, trimmed in green at the neck

Fluffy: red flannel nightgown, square yoke, trimmed in green

Fuzzy: red flannel snap-front one piece pajamas with elastic in the back, trimmed in green

Muffy: red flannel gown with a square yoke, green trim at the neck, one snap in the back, red bow** on her head

Muffy and Me™©: red flannel gown and scarf for little girls

**Bow is attached on factory dressed bear.

*Variations:
Alice's nightgown came in two different plaids.
Cornelius' ascot came with different background colors.

Muffy Valentine I

- White cotton eyelet dress with red ribbon sash, fastened with Velcro
- Red heart necklace
- Red headbow**

**Bow is attached on factory dressed bear.

Hangtag Note
Same size and design as Christening I

Cruisewear Collection
VanderBear Family Making Waves!

Early bears from this group were tush tag bears.

Cornelius: navy flannel double breasted blazer, red and white striped jersey, white trousers, classic captain's hat

Alice: white pleated middy dress in a cotton blend fabric, matching beret

Fluffy: navy and white sailor dress with matching beret

Fuzzy: navy and white sailor suit with matching beret

Muffy: navy sailor dress with a red & white stripe insert at the neck, white trim on collar, cuffs and hem, matching beret** with white trim and red pompon

Muffy and Me™©: sailor pinafore for girls from ages 2 to 8, with matching beret

*Family retired in 1988, Muffy in 1991.

✱*Variations:* Muffy's first dress was fastened with snaps, the second with Velcro. Some collars on the first version were knotted through a loop on the front of the dress. Later versions were tied in a bow with no loop.

Some variations of Cornelius came with a red hanky in his blazer pocket.

**A *few* hats were factory attached.

Muffy Trivia
Cornelius' boat was called the Merry Alice.

Hangtag Note
Blue print on a white tag. The first hangtag was large, the second was standard Muffy size.
A few of the early Muffys were issued with the same hangtag as Christening I.

Muffy Halloween I: Witch

- Orange dress with pattern of black stars and white dots, black satin at the hem, yolk and cuffs of coordinated black fabric with orange stars and white dots, fastened with one large snap in the back
- Black satin cape with tied collar
- Black velveteen witch's hat trimmed in satin
- Orange pumpkin fastened to cuff
- Black felt mask with elastic strap

Hangtag Note
Large 2" x 3" bright orange tag with "Muffy VanderBear" printed in black.

Taffeta: The Holiday Collection

VanderBear Family Holiday Limited Edition, limited to one year of production.

Cornelius: blue velveteen tuxedo with plaid lapels, white shirt; red bow tie, red cummerbund, and red boutonniere

Alice: elegant blue, green, and red plaid taffeta ball gown with puff sleeves; white eyelet ruffles on collar, cuffs, and hem; wide blue sash; separate eyelet trimmed petticoat; frilly net headpiece

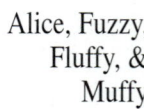

Fluffy: a miniature version of Alice, except for a ribbon and rosette on her head

Fuzzy: a miniature version of Cornelius

Muffy: the same blue, green, red plaid taffeta ball gown as Alice and Fluffy with snap back, eyelet trim, blue grosgrain ribbon sash; blue grosgrain bow with tiny red ribbon rose** on her head; one red ribbon rose with green ribbon trim on her skirt; separate eyelet trimmed petticoat with flower pot design at the hem*

*The same eyelet fabric was used for the first version of Muffy's **Day In The Country** apron.
**Bow is attached on factory dressed bear.

Alice, Fuzzy, Fluffy, & Muffy

A Day In The Country Collection

VanderBear Family

Cornelius: a country gentleman in denim overalls with plaid cuffs, sky-blue workshirt, plaid kerchief, straw hat

Alice: blue and white plaid dropwaisted dress, trimmed with a black bow and flowers, matching straw hat

Fluffy: denim pinafore, with eyelet trim and plaid pocket handkerchief, over a sky-blue eyelet trimmed blouse, straw hat trimmed with flowers

Fuzzy: denim overalls with blue and white plaid cuffs, a sky-blue workshirt, straw hat

Muffy: sky-blue smock dress, white eyelet apron, and straw hat trimmed with flowers and black band

Muffy and Me™©: Mother and daughter matching sky-blue cotton smock dresses

Family retired in 1989, Muffy in 1991.

Shown on the left is the first **Day In The Country** Muffy with "flower pot" design apron. Shown on right is the second **Day In The Country** Muffy. Behind both Muffys is the **Day In The Country Poster**, with the whole family pictured. Poster is described on page 22.

✳*Variations:*

First issue of Muffy's apron had a flower pot design at the hem (the same fabric as her Taffeta petticoat), second issue did not.

Flowers on the hat vary.

Hangtag Note
Some of the earliest versions of the Muffy with "flower pot" apron came with a large hangtag; later versions had a small hangtag.

The Nutcracker Suite Collection

VanderBear Family Holiday Limited Edition, limited to one year of production.

Cornelius: *The Majestic Toy Soldier* in royal blue and red with gold and blue ribbon trim crossing his chest, black hat with gold trim and blue plume, black ballet shoes

Alice: *The Enchanting Snowflake Queen* in pale blue satin and net, trimmed in silver with a silver crown, ballet shoes

Fluffy: *Young Clara at the Party*, in pink taffeta trimmed in black, pantaloons, white lace head piece with pink bow, black ballet shoes

Fuzzy: *The Handsome Prince* in light blue velveteen suit with knickers trimmed in black ribbon, eyelet cuffs, black ribbon tie, black ballet shoes

Muffy: *The Magical Sugar Plum Fairy* with 4 layers of plum and blue in her net skirt sprinkled with silver, plum satin leotard with snap and flowered neckline, silver crown**, plum ballet shoes**....her first pair of shoes!

**Crown and shoes are attached on factory dressed bear.

Hangtag Note First folded hangtag. White cover with blue border and nutcracker on the left. "Muffy VanderBear" and "Nutcracker Suite Collection" are printed in black. Inside you are welcomed to the performance with a brief history of the ballet and cast of characters. Yellow string was used instead of white.

VanderBear Hanger

Padded plush clothes hanger with bear head center

Out of it in Africa: The Safari Collection

VanderBear Family dressed in khaki with leopard print accents for an African adventure

Cornelius: safari hat and binoculars

Alice: net covered hat and compass on belt

Fluffy: safari hat and black panther on leash

Fuzzy: safari hat and canteen

Muffy: khaki jumper, leopard print scarf, hat with net, camera strapped to her wrist

Out Of It In Africa Chairs:** 20" rocker and 16" chair in natural wood with woven rattan seats

*Family retired in 1991, Muffy in 1992.

**Although the Chair and Rocker were not listed in the catalog as part of the Collection, they were pictured in the same catalog in a Safari setting containing a VanderBear hat and binoculars. Therefore, most collectors consider them accessories to the Collection.

❋*Variations:*

First Muffy had snaps, second had Velcro.

Alice's compass came in two sizes.

Hangtag Note
Leopard print border and lion with the first gold elastic cord. "Muffy VanderBear" and "Out of it in Africa" are printed in black.

19

Muffy Halloween II: Black Cat

2-piece black velour catsuit with orange stitching, mask

✶*Variations:*

First Issue: snap back, heavy glitter on mask
Second Issue: tie back, less glitter on mask
Third Issue: tie back, silver thread stitching on mask instead of glitter

Hangtag Note
Glitter Cats: First issued with large, pale orange hangtag with white string.
Later came with small, pale orange hangtag and white string.
Silver Stitched Cats: small, bright orange hangtag on gold elastic cord.
On all tags "Muffy VanderBear" was printed in black.

Furrier & Ives: The Skating Collection

VanderBear Family Holiday Limited Edition, an old-fashioned skating party, limited to one year of production.

Cornelius: Nordic sweater, red corduroy overalls with suspenders, black Cossack cap, black skates

Alice: "fur" trimmed red corduroy coat, plumed black hat, black muff, black skates

Fluffy: "fur" trimmed red corduroy coat with capelet, red beret, black muff, black skates

Fuzzy: black and green Nordic sweater, red corduroy overalls with suspenders, black Cossack hat, black skates

Muffy: red corduroy coat with gold buttons, white "fur" trimmed hat**, white "fur" muff with plaid ribbon around the muff and a red ribbon to go around her neck, white skates with plaid laces**

**Hats and skates are attached on factory dressed bear.

Hangtag Note
Black hangtag with silver border. "Muffy VanderBear," "Furrier & Ives," and "The Skating Party" are printed in white. Black string is used instead of white.

Muffy Trivia
Instructions were sent to dealers for restoring bent skate blades to their original condition by covering the blade with a damp towel and lightly pressing with a hot iron.

Muffy Valentine II

- Pink cotton dress with a double layered skirt in a tiny red heart print, heart-shaped buttons in back, collar trimmed in red satin, red ribbon sash, attached red net underskirt
- Red and pink double bow with pink rosette headbow**

**Bow is attached on factory dressed bear.

*Hangtag Note
The hangtag for Valentine II, Valentine III, and the Bunny are all the same, with only the words "Muffy VanderBear". Some were hung from the top and others from the end; the colors of the printing vary from pale lavender to pink.*

**1989-
1991**

Posters, *VanderBear Family*
**Day In The Country, Out of It In Africa, Nutcracker Suite,
Furrier and Ives, and later issue High Tea, 18" x 24", shrink-wrapped on cardboard**

**1989-
retired**

Muffy VanderBear Display

24-1/2" high x 8" deep, enclosed acrylic display case for 4 Muffys with a special section for hangtags, free-standing or wall-mounted

Muffy Bunny

- Muffy masquerades as a VanderBunny with her own Easter basket and a pink, 2-piece, velour bunny suit.

Variations: Muffy's first Easter basket was wicker, the second was plastic. Some of the first Bunnies came with a snap back, but most were tied.

Boutique Header, *VanderBear Family*

Laminated cardboard sign with easel or hanger back for display.
Spotlights VanderBears and VanderBear Wear, 12" x 16"

The High Tea Collection

VanderBear Family dressed for High Tea in the gardens of VanderBear Manor

Cornelius: pink trousers, paisley suspenders, stripe shirt with white collar and cuffs, black tie

Alice: pink floral print pleated tea dress with white organdy collar and pleated insert and cuffs, pearls, straw hat with black trim and rose

Fluffy: drop waist dress in same fabric as Alice, white organdy collar, pink bow on head

Fuzzy: pink knickers, sailor style stripe shirt

Muffy: blue and white gingham check pinafore with rose pattern, white organdy blouse with appliquéd flowers on collar, bloomers, straw hat** with black trim and pink bow

White Wicker Chairs: 7" for Muffy and 11" for Fluffy

High Tea Note Cards: gift package of 5 with envelopes, tied with bow

*Family retired in 1991, Muffy in 1992.
**Hat is attached on factory dressed bear.

Hangtag Note
Folded hangtag that "Requests the pleasure of your company at High Tea this afternoon in the gardens of VanderBear Manor".

❋*Variation:* A few of the first Muffy **High Teas** had a snap on the pinafore and a button on the blouse; later, both the pinafore and the blouse were fastened with Velcro.

Muffy Pilgrim

- Black pilgrim dress with eyelet hem, white cuffs and collar, belt with buckle
- White pilgrim bonnet with ribbon tie
- Felt turkey with ribbon leash

✳*Variations:*

Some early versions came without belt and buckle, shown on left, but were made available to anyone who contacted North American Bear Company.

First belt buckles were different types of silver leatherette; later ones are silver plastic, shown on right.

Eyelet trim also varies.

Trunk

Red plaid trunk with Muffy decal on the front, included clothing bar, two small hangers, and accessory drawer, 10" x 6" x 5".

Variations:

First Trunk: starburst design on its interior (not shown)

Second trunk: plain interior with red metal edging on two sides of top and bottom; sold separately or with a bare Muffy, Tree Trim outfit, and a Furrier and Ives outfit; shown on left (Original outfits packaged in trunks came without hangers and headers.)

Third trunk: interior printed with Muffy's signature, slightly smaller than the previous trunks, different plaid in a lighter shade with red metal edging on all four sides of top and bottom and a newly designed handle; sold separately or with a bare Muffy, Sweet Dreams outfit, and a Back to School outfit; shown on right (Original outfits packaged in trunks came without hangers and headers.).

Rare: solid red trunk with decal and starburst interior issued for a short time before first plaid version was available.

25

The Tree Trimming Collection

VanderBear Family Holiday Limited Edition, Christmas at home, limited to one year of production

Cornelius: black watch-plaid jacket and twill pants, candy stripe dickey, holiday bow tie, monogrammed velvet slippers

Alice: lace-trimmed robe, Christmas tree earrings, corduroy slippers

Fluffy: black watch-plaid dress with candy cane trim, organdy apron, matching headbow, Mary Jane shoes

Fuzzy: plaid rompers and Christmas bow tie

Muffy: white organdy pinafore with red trim and candy cane appliqué on collar, red and white candy-striped cotton smock dress, green and red plaid head bow**, gingerbread cookie charm sewn into her pocket (**first charm of her collection**), and her first pair of Mary Jane shoes - red

Scottie VanderDog: 4" black plush puppy in a red cardboard kennel with a green plaid bow, FD only

Muffy's Christmas Tree I: 9" tree with gingerbread ornaments, glass balls, tiny presents, white ribbon, baby's breath, red garland, and apples - according to NABCO only 15,000 were made *(See Variations on next page.)*

The Tree Trimming Collection

Muffy's Cookie Plate: 3 little gingerbread cookies arranged on a red and green holly plate, packaged in cellophane with header

VanderBear Family Sofa: green moiré camel-back sofa, 34"W x 19"H x 19"D

**Bow is attached on factory dressed bear.

❋Variations:

Shown below: two of ***many*** variations of the Tree Trimming Christmas Tree

The Tree on the left has 4 gingerbread ornaments that are fastened to the tree by a loop on their heads. The base is the same on all four sides.

The Tree on the right has 6 gingerbread ornaments, but only 1 is fastened to the tree with a loop on its head, the other 5 are glued onto the tree. The base has a different Santa picture on each side.

> *Hangtag Note*
> *Folded hangtag opens to reveal a Holiday letter from the VanderBears. Their new settee for the drawing room is mentioned as well as Muffy's new puppy.*

Muffy Trivia

Scottie VanderDog was pictured in the 1989 catalog with a solid green bow, but it was plaid when he arrived. The Spring 1990 catalog pictures Scottie with a leash, but it was never produced...perhaps that is why he ran away in the summer of 1990.

Muffy Angel

- Holiday Boxed Limited Edition
- Heavenly Blue gown sprinkled with stars and trimmed with gold, separate gold petticoat
- Embossed foil wings and halo with stars
- Hand-tied into an ornate Renaissance-style box with Certificate of Authenticity on inside cover
- Factory Dressed only

Muffy Trivia
Muffy wore her Italian Renaissance Angel costume for her kindergarten Holiday Play. Even though the catalog showed Muffy's halo without stars, they all came with stars.

Hangtag Note
The bottom line reads,
"Limited Holiday Edition 1989."

Greeting/Christmas Cards

Boxed sets with 20 cards and 21 envelopes, *Furrier & Ives, Tree Trimming, Muffy Angel*

1989 Greeting Cards; 1992 Pop-up cards; 1992 Holiday Stickers, Gift Tags, and Sticker Book. See descriptions on page 55 & 63.

Muffy Valentine III

- Heart-strewn romper with pink rick-rack trim, tied in back
- Pink Mary Janes
- Pink headbow**
- Valentine card tied to her wrist

**Bow is attached on factory dressed bear.*

✳*Variations:*
Background colors vary between cream, and white.

Early versions came with darker pink shoes.

1990
MUFFY & FUZZY issued undressed for Valentine's Day with red Valentine ribbons and tags

Hangtag Note
The same hangtag was used for Valentine II and Bunny, see page 22.

Muffy St. Patrick's Day

White cotton dress with green shamrock print, eyelet trimmed hem, green check cuffs and collar, green check bloomers, green check headbow**, green Mary Janes

**Bow is attached on factory dressed bear.*

✳*Variations:*
Check trim on earlier Muffys was larger and yellowish green, the newer version is smaller and bright green.

Eyelet trim also varies.

Hangtag Note
Special hangtag gives Muffy the Irish name of "Muffeen."

Muffy Trivia
Muffy's dress was sent to her by friends in Ireland to wear in the St. Patrick's Day Parade.

Muffy Chick

Easter playsuit in yellow velour with chick head cap and wings tied with orange ribbon, orange Mary Janes

Variations:
Old and new versions came with gold beaks; the middle came with a yellow beak.

First issued without black stitching all the way around the eyes, shown on left.

- -

1990-
1998

Muffy Beach

Muffy: red print cotton bikini, matching kerchief, white monogrammed terry cloth towel (outfit packaged with Muffy cutout)

Deck Chair and Umbrella:
red and white stripe chair with monogrammed umbrella, packaged with header

Variations:
First issued with snap on back of bikini top; later issued with all elastic.

The first and latest versions of the deck chair fabric have narrow woven stripes that are the same color of red on both the top and underneath. A version in the middle had wider and brighter red stripes on a more open weave fabric that was printed on the top side only.

Muffy Trivia
Muffy wore her new bathing suit on the beach in France during the family's trip to Gibearny.

Gibearny: An Impressionist Collection

VanderBear Family, inspired by their visit to the French gardens of Gibearny made famous by Monet's impressionistic Water Lily paintings

Cornelius: artist's smock, dickey, cravat, hanky, corduroy pants, straw hat, pince-nez glasses

Alice: flowered voile dress with organdy collar, water lily headpiece

Fluffy: floral print dress with organdy collar, Mary Janes, water lily headpiece

Fuzzy: 2 piece linen sailor suit, rubber frog

Muffy: floral smock, lavender pinafore, lavender Mary Janes, water lily headpiece**, paint tube charm (with "Muffy" on it) sewn into her pocket (*second charm in her collection*), palette on her paw

Garden Bench: rustic wooden French bench with rattan covered arms and seat, 21" x 17" x 9"

**Headpiece is attached on factory dressed bear.*

Variation:
Cornelius' first hat was more flat with rolled brim. Later hats were rounded without rolled brim.

Earlier Muffys <u>might</u> have had a button, but most were fastened with Velcro.

Back To School

Muffy: black and white number-print dress with white trim, red beret, red Mary Janes, school bag

Hoppy, Muffy's new friend is introduced: red and white number-print dress with white trim, black beret, black Mary Janes, school bag

Watches: black and red watch with Muffy's picture, red or black strap, gift box

School Desk: red wooden desk with Muffy's signature on the front, 7" x 5" x 6"

Notebook: old-fashioned red and black notebook with Muffy illustration on the front, black ribbon ties, 5" x 6-3/4"

*Muffy's Desk retired in 1992, the remainder of the collection retired in 1993.

Muffy Trivia

Hoppy became Muffy's "bosom bunny". Hoppy's parents travel a lot (which is not unusual for a family of rabbits). When they are gone, Hoppy stays with the VanderBears and joins them in many of their adventures.

Remembearances:
A Wedding Collection

A romantic glance backwards...

Cornelius: black tails, pique dickey and vest, cravat, top hat

Alice: white moiré taffeta, lace and tulle bridal ensemble; garter; bouquet

> *Hangtag Note*
> *Oval insert on gold tag printed with "Remembearances" and either Alice or Cornelius' name.*

Stationery, *VanderBear*

Each gift packaged with 5 cards and 5 envelopes: *Day in the Country, Gibearny, Remembearance, High Tea* (*High Tea Stationery* was first issued as note cards with the *High Tea Collection* in 1989.)

Sweet Dreams:
The Victorian Sleepwear Collection

VanderBear Family dressed in old-fashioned nightwear

Cornelius: monogrammed nightshirt and cap

Alice: peignoir and sleepcap

Fluffy: lace-tucked gown and cap

Fuzzy: monogrammed shirt and nightcap

Muffy: pajamas and bed jacket tied with satin ribbon, satin ribbon around her head**

Muffy's Teddy Bear: 3" brown felt bear with red plaid bow in red shopping bag, packaged in cellophane with header

The family and Muffy's Teddy Bear retired in 1992, Muffy in 1993.
**Ribbon is attached on factory dressed bears.*

✳*Variations:*

First issue was in thin cotton.

Second issue was a cotton blend with less wrinkles.

Lace also varies.

Hangtag Note
White tag with very thin gold cord. Both "Muffy VanderBear" and "Sweet Dreams" are printed in pale blue.

Muffy Trivia
Alice makes secret milk (warm milk and honey) for Fluffy, Fuzzy, and Muffy at bedtime.

Musical Soireé:
The Purple Velvet Collection

VanderBear Family Holiday Limited Edition, celebrating a musical Victorian Christmas at home

Cornelius: white tie, breeches and tails, damask waistcoat, lace cuffs

Alice: décolleté evening gown with lavender bows, purple choker, feathered headdress, bouquet of flowers

Fluffy: velvet dress, white lace trimmed collar, lavender sash with rose, lavender headbow

Fuzzy: Little Lord "Fauntlebear" velvet suit

Muffy: velvet smock dress with white pique collar and cuffs, lavender ribbon rose, ribboned pantaloons, purple Mary Janes, plaid headbow**

Musical Soireé Christmas Tree II: 18" Victorian fir; trumpet, French horn, and violin ornaments; musical stave paper base; purple ribbons and bows; baby's breath; plastic display box

Chaise Lounge: purple moiré settee, black tassels and trim, no back, 16" x 35" x 16"

Muffy's Stradibearius: 5" wooden violin in purple illustrated box with cellophane window. "Muffy VanderBear" and "Stradibearius" are printed on the box

*Family retired in 1991, Stradibearius, Chaise Lounge, and Tree in 1990, Muffy in 1992.
**Bow is attached on factory dressed bears.

✳Variations:

The tag on the inside of Muffy's first dress is printed "Vintage Collection," later changed to "Musical Soiree."

The fabric and lace on Muffy's dress vary.

> **Muffy Trivia**
> Muffy took violin lessons from Madam Bearloska.

> *Hangtag Note
> Ivory tag with purple border and music motif. "Muffy VanderBear" and "Musical Soiree" are printed in purple.*

Muffy Little
Fir Tree

- Holiday Boxed Limited Edition
- Organdy and satin, red and
  green tree-inspired dress
- Star and holly headdress, attached
- Green satin slippers
- "Partridge in a Bear Tree" on
  right paw
- Victorian style gift box
  with certificate of authenticity
  on the back
- Factory Dressed only

Muffy Trivia
Muffy's Fir Tree
costume was for
the Teddy Bear
Fancy Dress Ball.

1990

Armoire

- Country-style wood with top shelf
  and 2 bottom drawers, 16-1/2" x
  13-1/2" x 7-3/4"

❋*Variations:*
Both the Armoire and Sleigh Bed were issued
  in a variety of different wood shades,
  according to availability. Early issues
  were much lighter.
The plaque or decal on the foot of the bed and
  on the front of the Armoire also varies.

Shown: Muffy's Bed and Armoire
Bedding Accessories (introduced in 1991)
First Armoire Accessories (introduced in 1991)

1990

Sleigh Bed

Wood with monogram at the foot: comes with white mattress and lace-trimmed pillow with embroidered monogram, 6" x 14-1/2" x 7-1/2"

**1990-
1995**

Muffy VanderBear Club Membership Kit

Members receive a ribbon-tied portfolio containing Membership Card and Certificate, **Back to School** Stationery, Muffy Logo Pendant, 10 Stickers, and a Photo Album of Muffy's Collections. Also included is a subscription to Muffy's own newsletter, *Fanfare*, published 3 times a year. New Muffy VanderBear Club Kit available in 1996, contains linen covered Collection Album, see page 86. Original Kit pictured on page 126.

Mommy and Me:
The Teacup Collection

Mother and daughter tea party

Alice: blue print teacup and pansy print dress with shawl collar, organza headbow, nosegay of flowers on her wrist

Muffy: the same print dress with yellow accents, organza headbow**, yellow Mary Janes, a card for mother tied to her wrist that says "I Love You, xxoo, Muffy"

Frame: ribbon and pansy motif on resin frame with a picture of Muffy, 2-3/4" x 3-1/4", boxed in white VdB logo box with plastic cover

Tea Set: personalized Muffy-size tea set with pansy motif, 12 pieces, box is illustrated with picture of collection

Teatime Settee: wicker garden settee, blue tea cup print cushion with pink piping, 17" x 11"

Teatime Table: wicker with blue accent, 5" x 7" in diameter

Teatime Chair: wicker, blue accent, blue teacup print cushion with pink piping, 7"

**Bow is attached on factory dressed bear.

Hangtag Note
White tag with triple border and pansy at the top. "Muffy VanderBear" and "The Teacup Collection" are printed in blue.

Muffy Trivia
For Mother's Day, Muffy plans a tea party and serves Alice tea in the garden. Muffy's gift to Alice was a framed photo of herself. Pictured in the catalog are plain fabric cushions with teacup piping on the chair and settee. According to NABCO only a few of these were made.

Easter Fantasy

Muffy: pink organdy pinafore with embroidered butterfly and flower basket on her pocket, bloomers, hemp Easter bonnet** with flowers, basket with chick tied to her wrist

Hoppy: yellow organdy pinafore with embroidered carrot pocket, bloomers, bonnet with carrots, basket with bunny on her wrist

**Hat is attached on factory dressed bear. Butterfly for photo only.

✻*Variations: Last issue of Muffy wore a lighter pink pinafore and her hat had a hemp hat band.*

> *Hangtag Note*
> *White background with pale pink and green borders.*
> *"Muffy VanderBear" and "Easter Fantasy" are printed*
> *in pale pink.*

The Wild West: A Traveling Rodeo Show

VanderBear Family goes West!

Cornelius, *Paw*: fringed jacket, jeans, bandanna, cowboy hat

Alice, *Ma*: chambray poke bonnet, bandanna print dress

Fluffy, *Pawcahontas*: Indian princess in fringed dress and feathered headdress

Fuzzy, *The Kid*: chaps, western shirt, bandanna, cowboy hat

Muffy, *Miss Muffy*: red gingham dress, bandanna print smock with blue chambray hankie sewn in front pocket, cowboy hat, red Mary Janes

Oatsie: 9" spotted Appaloosa one-trick pony, Muffy's newest friend, issued factory dressed only in western gear, western outfit was never issued separately.

Hangtag Note
Folded hangtag is an advertisement for "The VanderBear Traveling Wild West Show" and gives "Miss Muffy" the title of "The Littlest Cowpoke." Inside you are invited to "step right up" and Oatsie "the wonder pony" is introduced.

Muffy Trivia
"Hopp-a-long" Hoppy could not go to the *Wild West* because she had Rocky Mountain Spring Fever. Even though the catalog pictured Muffy in boots, she only wore red Mary Janes.

Paw de Deux
Ballerinas at ballet class

Muffy: tutu, pink leotard, pink ballet shoes**, flowered headband**
Hoppy: tutu, blue leotard, blue ballet shoes, headbow

**Headband and shoes are attached on factory dressed bear.*

*Hangtag Note
White background with pink and blue border. "Muffy VanderBear" and "Paw de Deux" are printed in pink.*

✳*Variation:* Later outfits packaged on Muffy and Hoppy cutouts, color varies.

Armoire Accessories

Muffy's signature blue fabric-covered closet set: hatbox, shoe chest (for 4 pairs), and four fabric hangers, boxed. *Accessories pictured on page 36.*

Underthings

- Muffy and Hoppy
- Each set includes teddy, bloomers, and panties; packaged as outfits only on Muffy and Hoppy cutouts, with headers and hangers.
- No hangtag included.

Bedding Accessories

Muffy's signature blue fabric bed set: pillow, pillow case, sheet, and quilt, packaged with header and Muffy cutout. *Accessories pictured on page 36.*

The Fortune Tellers

Magical costumes for Halloween

Muffy Gypsy: peasant-style paisley dress, satin stripe apron with gold coins, matching vest and slippers**, gypsy headscarf with attached golden earrings

Hoppy Genie: fringed midriff top, brocade bloomers with golden coins, feathered turban, slippers with curled toes

Fortune Telling Accessories: crystal ball, bearot cards, magic lamp, "flying" carpet, boxed

**Slippers are attached on factory dressed bear.*

The Ballet Recital

Muffy: tulle and satin recital costume, sparkling toe shoes, silvery crown,
pink flowers tied to her paw

Hoppy: similar to Muffy's costume with different trims and purple flowers in her paw

✳*Variation:* Later outfits
packaged on Muffy
and Hoppy cutouts.

Hangtag Note
White background with lavender border. "Muffy
VanderBear" and ' Ballet Recital" are in lavender.

Muffy Trivia
Muffy and Hoppy's first
dance performance was
"Chopawniana."

Muffy Postcard & Button I

With original Muffy portrait logo
Logo and postcard are pictured on page 127.

Muffy SnowBear

- Holiday Boxed Limited Edition
- Fluffy white snowsuit with "coal" buttons
- Carrot nose
- Plaid scarf
- Twig Broom
- Black hat with cardinal and sprig of holly
- Illustrated box (reminiscent of a Victorian Christmas Card) with certificate of authenticity on the back
- Factory Dressed only

Muffy Trivia
Muffy wore her Snowbear costume to go caroling.

Hangtag Note
White background with slate blue border. "Muffy VanderBear" and "SnowBear" are printed in the same blue color.

Bal Masqué:
The Legendary Party Collection

VanderBear Family Holiday masqueraders at the Commedia Dell'Arte Ball in a 16th Century** Italian Comedy

Cornelius: "Gilles" in white satin, crimson bows on his slippers, ruffled collar, hat, mask

Alice: "Pierrette" in harlequin print Panier-style dress, ruffled collar, black satin slippers, feather tricorn hat, mask

Fluffy: "Columbine" in harlequin print dress, black satin slippers, feathered tricorn hat, mask

Fuzzy: "Harlequin" in ruffled collared jacket with pompons, matching pants, black satin slippers, feathered tricorn hat, mask

Muffy: "Infanta" in gold-trimmed pink moiré taffeta gown with peplum, floral ribbon sash with gold bow, black shoes with laces, floral feathered headbow, mask on stick

Hoppy: "Lapina" in gold-trimmed blue moiré taffeta gown with ruffled collar, floral ribbon sash with gold bow, black shoes with laces, floral feathered head piece, mask on stick

Oatsie: "Octavio" in collar and mask, *the first time Oatsie was available both dressed and undressed.* Oatsie is described on page 39.

Bal Masque Recamier: magenta pink moiré fainting couch, 37" x 16" x 16"

* *Family and Recaimer retired in 1992; Muffy, Hoppy, & Oatsie in 1993. Bal Masque was the first Hoppy and Oastie to retire.*
** *16th Century is used in the catalog, but the tag reads 17th Century.*

Hangtag Note
Folded fan-shaped hangtag on wrist with tassel, inside is an invitation to the ball.

Muffy Butterfly

First Boxed Limited Edition of 10,000 to commemorate the formation of the Muffy VanderBear Club, for Club members only

- Blue velvet and gold net butterfly suit with gold ruffled collar, jewels, and ribbons
- Blue and green felt wings with gold painted veins
- Blue velvet slippers with a jewel on each curled and pointed toe
- Blue velvet cap with jewels, antennae, and gold tie
- Crystal wand with butterflies, ribbons, and flowers tied to right paw
- Presentation box with butterfly wing opening
- Certificate of Authenticity with LE number
- Factory Dressed only

> *Hangtag Note*
> *Round blue tag with "Muffy VanderBear," "Butterfly," and the border in gold.*

Muffy Trivia

It was announced in the Winter 1990 issue of the *North American Bear* News that there would be a special LE Muffy available at a Muffy Convention planned for May 1991 in Chicago. The theme of the Convention was to have been *Muffy's Midsummer Night's Dream*. However in the following issue of the NABCO *News*, the Convention was cancelled and that special LE Muffy became the first Club Piece–*Muffy Butterfly*!

Down On The Farm

Muffy: blue and white checked sundress with floral borders, kerchief, blue shoes with yellow laces, sack of *Muffy's Farm Feed* tied to wrist

Muffy's Farm Friends: Patti The Cow, Mary The Lamb, Rudy The Pig, Lucy The Goose, Webster The Duck in gingham bows, factory dressed only

Farm Cart: rustic wooden cart with Muffy's signature on the back, 10-3/4" x 4-1/2" x 4-1/2"

*The Farm Cart was retired in the Spring of 1997, but was sold out before the end of 1996.

❋*Variations:*

The wheels on the first cart (shown on left) were hand crafted, while the second cart (shown on right), has die cut wheels.

According to the catalog and *NABCO News*, Muffy's first shoes had pale green laces.

Muffy Trivia
The farm that Muffy visits belongs to her mother's friend "Aunt Beatrice" in the "Bearkshires".

Dutch Treat

Muffy: delft blue print dress, cap with golden braids, red tulip in left paw, hand-carved wooden shoes

Hoppy: delft blue pantaloons and smock, white flowers on bodice, cap with braids, hand-carved wooden shoes

Hangtag Note
Round tag with blue and yellow border. "Muffy VanderBear" and "Dutch Treat" are printed in blue.

Muffy Mail

Gift Enclosure with envelopes in 3 designs: Muffy Cherub, Hoppy Cherub, Hoppy and Muffy Friendship

Greeting Cards with envelopes in 3 designs: Muffy and Hoppy Heart, Muffy and Dove, Muffy and Oatsie

Stationery Set, notepaper with envelopes, package of 8 each in 2 designs: Muffy and Dove, Hoppy and Muffy Friendship

Postcard Set, portfolio of 9 cards, 3 each of: Muffy and Oatsie; Muffy and Hoppy Cherubs; Muffy, Hoppy and Oatsie with cart

Sticker Book: 24 stickers in above designs

Counter Display Unit for Muffy Mail is 11" x 9" x 7"

Cherry Pie: The Baking Collection

"Daddy and Me at Patisserie V de B"

Cornelius: monogrammed toque blanc (chef's hat), apron, plaid shirt, green pants, quilted oven mitt

Muffy: cherry print dress with plaid collar and white eyelet apron with cherry embroidered pocket, quilted potholder** tied to her wrist, red shoes, green headbow**

Pie Cupboard: cherry motifs and Muffy's signature on white wooden pie safe with mesh windows, 11" x 6" x 3"

Cherry Pie: cherry pie with Muffy's signature pricked in crust, boxed in "VdeB Patisserie" bakery box, 2-3/4" diameter x 3/4" thick

*Bow is atttached on factory dressed bear
*Potholder is atttached on factory dressed bear

Picnic Collection

1992-1996*

VanderBear Family picnic outing in VanderBear Woods

Cornelius: chambray shorts, "goin' fishin" print shirt, checked ascot, pork-pie hat, fishing creel with hangtag, 3-1/2" x 5" x 4"

Alice: checked porch dress with white pique napkin print cuffs and pocket flaps, straw and fabric hat

Fluffy: checked sundress with white pique napkin print trim, bouquet on bodice, peek-a-boo hat

Fuzzy: chambray overalls, checked cuffs, "goin' fishin" shirt, 10" bamboo fishing pole with fish

Muffy: checked sundress with white pique collar and pocket flaps with berry print accents, straw picture bonnet with meadow flowers

Tablecloth Set: floral and checked "VdeB" monogrammed tablecloth, 21" x 21", and 4 matching napkins, 8" x 8", packaged with header and hangtag

*Picnic Set: cardboard box printed in wicker design, 4-1/2" x 1-1/2 " x 3-1/2": 4 tiny 3-1/4" spoons, 4 printed tin 3-1/8" plates, and 13" x 13" signature tablecloth

* The Picnic Set, which was originally supposed to be packaged in a wicker basket, retired in 1993, but was sold out before the end of 1992. Family retired Spring 1995, Muffy retired Spring 1996.

Muffy Trivia
Hoppy missed the picnic because of a terrible case of the sniffles.

Hangtag Note
Folded Hangtag

Rainy Day

Muffy: bright yellow rain slicker, Sou'western hat, red and yellow boots

Hoppy: blue slicker with hood, blue and yellow boots

Rainy Day Umbrella: personalized, packaged with header

Rainy Day Puzzle: introduced in the 1993 Spring catalog, 221 pieces, boxed, 14" x 10" when completed

* Due to production problems, this collection was not available in stores until 1993.

❋*Variation:*

The first versions of the raincoats were shiny, slick fabric. Later versions were a heavier fabric with more texture. This later version of Muffy's slicker was also a lighter yellow. Muffy's first raincoat also had an unfinished hem, but in 1996 her raincoat was stitched at the hem.

Hangtag Note
Blue tag with "Muffy VanderBear" in yellow and "Rainy Day" in white.

- -

Scarf
Life Is One Big Dress Up

First renewal gift for Muffy VanderBear Club second year members, pink cotton scarf featuring Muffy in 16 outfits, 20-1/2" x 20-1/2". *Pictured on page 126.*

Yankee Doodle

Red, white, and blue Fourth of July finery
Muffy Yankee Doodle: colonial frock, feathered tricorn hat**, ribbon lace-up red shoes
Hoppy Uncle Sam: top hat, rompers, tails, bow tie, ribbon lace-up black shoes

**Hat is attached on factory dressed bear.

Eine Kliene Mountain Climbin':
The Alpine Collection

VanderBear Family Holiday in the Alps with traditional Tyrolean folk costumes.

Cornelius: felt vest with woven trim and painted wooden buttons, pique peasant shirt, felt lederhosen with embroidered VdeB logo, plaid tie, felt hat with feather

Alice: dirndl dress with plaid shawl, felt hat with feather and bird

Fluffy: dirndl dress with pique bodice, plaid apron, felt hat with bird

Fuzzy: lederhosen, painted wooden buttons, suspenders, peasant blouse, print tie, hat with feather

Muffy: green felt jacket, red felt skirt, Alpine floral braid, felt hat with plaid ribbon and feather

Hoppy: felt jacket and skirt with floral braid, felt braided hat

Oatsie: felt blanket, hat, ribbon reins

Muffy's Alpine Sleigh: wooden, edelweiss motif, personalized, 12" x 9" x 5"

Muffy's Alpine Tree: bird & bell ornaments, cuckoo clocks, edelweiss, woven ribbon trim, bluebird on top (signifies happiness and good fortune), 10", boxed

* Family retired in 1993; Muffy, Hoppy, Oatsie, and accessories in 1994.

❋*Variation:* First sleigh came with green runners, second had red runners.

*Hangtag Note
Folded Hangtag. First Hoppys issued with hangtag that said "Hoppy VanderBear" instead of "VanderHare." This was later corrected.*

Muffy Trivia
Cornelius built the Alpine Sleigh for Muffy.

Muffy GingerBear

- Holiday Boxed Limited Edition
- Cookie outfit in brown velour with white "icing" and "gumdrop" buttons
- Gingerbread recipe card tied to wrist
- Gingerbread house gift box with instructions and patterns for making a Muffy cookie house, with certificate of authenticity on the back
- Factory Dressed only

Muffy Trivia
Muffy wore her Gingerbread costume to perform at the Chalet during the family's Alpine Adventure.

Ornaments

First 4 of a series of hand painted resin ornaments based on limited edition Muffys
Angel, Little Fir Tree, SnowBear, GingerBear: 2-1/2" x 3", boxed

Series of 14
ornaments
issued
between 1992
and 1994

Holiday Gift Tags & Stickers

Featuring Muffy, Hoppy, and Oatsie: 8 gift tags, 3" x 3-1/2", packaged with header and 24 stickers packaged with header. *Tags and Stickers are pictured on page 28.*

Pop-Up Cards

Old fashioned diecut, 4" x 6-1/2" with envelope in cellophane bag, *Sweet Dreams, Furrier & Ives, Musical Soiree, Tree Trimming. Cards are pictured on page 28. Catalog lists **Bal Masque**, but this was not produced as a Pop-up card.*

Kyoto Blossoms

In honor of the annual Japanese celebration of the Cherry Blossom Festival in Kyoto

Muffy: blue kimono with cherry blossom motif, obi sash, matching headbow** with flowers

Hoppy: cherry pink kimono with the same design as Muffy's, obi sash, matching headbow with flowers

Kyoto Blossom Accessories: "pokuri" (traditional Japanese sandals) washi paper fan, a fabric bag that matches their obi sashes, packaged in an authentic "tomoebako" box

* *Although part of the 1993 Spring Collection, Kyoto blossoms was available in the stores in November of 1992.*

***Bow is attached on factory dressed bear.*

Flower Festival

1993- 1995*

A May Day celebration in the Wildflower Garden of VanderBear Manor to introduce *Muffy's new rabbit friends, Bud and Rose*

Muffy: pink dotted Swiss dress with floral trim, pink bloomers, flower garland headband**

Hoppy: aqua dotted Swiss dress with floral trim, aqua bloomers, flower garland headbow

Muffy's Flower Festival Friends: Oatsie, Lucy the Goose, Mary the Lamb, Patti the Cow, Rudy the Pig, Webster the Duck, Bud, Rose, all with floral garlands

Flower Garlands: for Muffy's friends (accept for Bud and Rose) with instructions, packaged with header

> **Muffy Trivia**
> Bud and Rose are Hoppy's cousins.

**Bud and Rose were not retired with the rest of the Collection. Factory dressed Muffy, Muffy outfit, and Hoppy outfit were sold out before the end of 1994.*

***Garland is attached on factory dressed bear.*

VdBeekeeping Collection
A Taste O' Honey

VanderBear Family on their honey farm

Cornelius: black and white cotton ticking overalls with beehive pocket label and beehive bordered neckerchief

Alice: striped ticking pinafore with beehive pocket label and floral bordered scarf

Fluffy: striped ticking pinafore with bee pocket label on bodice, floral bordered neckerchief

Fuzzy: ticking overalls with bee pocket label, beehive bordered neckerchief

Muffy Bumble Bee: velvety striped romper with daisy on bodice, felt antennae and embroidered wings attached to hood, black Mary Janes

Hoppy Ladybug: black velvety jumpsuit, felt antennae, scalloped collar and spotted felt ladybug wing attached to hood, red Mary Janes

Large Honey Jar: porcelain with floral motif, Muffy Bumble Bee on lid, 6" wooden dipper with ladybug handle, 6-1/4" x 5-1/4", boxed

Small Honey Jar: porcelain with Muffy's name written in leaves, bee on lid, 3-3/4" wooden dipper with lady bug handle, 3-1/2" x 3", boxed

Sticker Book: 50 stickers that tell the story of *The VdBeeKeeping Tale*

Family retired Fall 1996; Muffy, Hoppy, Honey Jars, and Sticker Book retired 1997.

✳*Variation:*

Muffy's bee wings were made of a finer and whiter fabric in the later versions.

Hangtag Note
Folded hangtag in the shape of a beehive.

Sewing Lesson Collection

Fluffy helps Muffy and Hoppy make aprons.

Fluffy: pique pinafore, stripe dress, tape measure headbow

Muffy: yellow smocked dress in custom printed fabric, tied in back; yellow tape measure headbow**, spring green new style T-strap shoes

Hoppy: lavender smock in custom fabric with front Velcro closing, lavender tape measure headbow, coral pink T-strap shoes

Collectors Thimbles: 3 porcelain thimbles with a portrait of each (Fluffy, Hoppy, and Muffy) in box covered with Muffy's yellow dress fabric, box: 2" x 4" x 2-1/4", thimbles: 1-1/8" x 1"

Muffy's Sewing Tin: double-handled tin with fabric to make 2 aprons for Muffy and Hoppy, pattern with Muffy's instructions, 4 scissors and thimble buttons on card, hangtag, 3" x 3-1/2" x 2-5/16"

**Bow is attached on factory dressed bear.

Horsin' Around:
The Equestrienne Collection

Muffy: black English style riding jacket, eyelet dickey, white jodhpurs with "chamois" inserts, laced paddock boots, top hat with organza bow

Hoppy: riding coat, dickey, khaki jodhpurs with "chamois" inserts, laced paddock boots, derby hat with organza bow

Oatsie: jockey cap with bow, bridle, leatherette saddle with gold monogram and red ribbon tie

---

VanderBear Family in New Fur

It more closely matches the original golden tan fur.

Tote Bag

2nd renewal gift for Muffy Club 3rd year members: blue bordered canvas bag with colorful Muffys & fans, 12-1/2" x 10-1/2" x 3". *Bag is pictured on page 126.*

Birthday Card I

From Muffy to Club members: accordion folded Muffy cutouts. *Card is pictured on page 127.*

Travels with Muffy: The Grand Tour Collection

Muffy: twill coat with plaid buttons, velvet collar and cuffs, passport tied into her pocket, velvety shoes and hat with plaid ribbon

Muffy Travel Diary: travel notes on back, 200 pages, 6-1/4" x 6-1/4"

Muffy Travel Watch: Muffy on top of the world, her hat is the second hand, navy blue band in tin case

Lulu

A 5" Scottish MacFluff with plaid neckbow, FD only

Lulu's Bed: tartan, personalized

Lulu's Brush: wooden, red strap

Lulu's Bowl: red tin, personalized

Lulu's Tag & Leash: red leash and personalized dog tag

Note: All accessories are packaged on headers.

Hangtag Note
Single tag in the Highland Fling crest shape with "Muffy's Dog Lulu" printed in yellow. This original tag was replaced on Lulu in 1996.

Muffy Trivia
Muffy found Lulu on the grounds of MacVanderBearn Castle.

A Highland Fling:
The Scottish Collection

VanderBear Family Holiday in Scotland at MacVanderBearn Castle

Cornelius: gold trimmed velveteen jacket, ribbon necktie with thistle accent, thistle corduroy vest with VdeB buttons, Malcolm tartan kilt, dickey, Scottish hat, argyle socks, gillie shoes

Alice: cutaway jacket with insignia buttons, lace jabot with thistle, velveteen skirt, Scottish hat, gillie shoes

Fluffy: argyle sweater, fringed Malcolm tartan skirt, tam, argyle socks, gillie shoes

Fuzzy: argyle sweater, velveteen pantaloons, Scottish hat, argyle socks, gillie shoes

Muffy: red sweater, Malcolm tartan skirt with fringed hem and front sporran pocket with tassel, tartan sash, corduroy tam** with pompon and yellow ribbon, argyle socks, gillie shoes

Hoppy: yellow sweater with thistle, fringed tartan circle skirt with pocket, velveteen pantaloons, tam, gillies

Snowdome: among the ruins of the castle tower, boxed, 6" x 18" around

Wreath: 12" with Scottish ornaments, boxed

Stocking: quilted illustrations, 12" x 8", packaged with header

* The Family, Snowdome, Wreath, and Stocking retired in 1994, Muffy and Hoppy retired in 1995.
**Tam is attached on factory dressed bear.

Hangtag Note
Folded

Muffy Trivia
The family wears kilts in the Malcolm plaid, Cornelius' Uncle's clan.

Muffy Snowflake

- Holiday Boxed Limited Edition
- Silvery snowflake costume with snowflake pattern cut into jacket and velvet skirt with silver snowflakes
- Sparkling net underskirt
- Snowflake crown, attached
- Iridescent wand
- Illustrated ice palace box with certificate of authenticity on the back
- Factory Dressed only

*Variation: Fabric color of Muffy's velvet skirt varies between white and cream.

Hangtag Note Sky blue tag with snowflake motif. "Muffy VanderBear" and "Snowflake" are in purple.

Muffy Trivia Fluffy made the Snowflake costume for Muffy to wear at a performance at MacVanderBearn Castle during their holiday in Scotland.

Ornaments, Racks, Stands, Stickers, Signs

ORNAMENTS, 2nd series of resin holiday ornaments based on Family Holiday Collections: *Bal Masque, Red Flannel, Furrier and Ives, Musical Soiree, Nutcracker, Tree Trimming*, 2-1/2" to 3", boxed. *Ornaments are pictured on page 55.*

Boutique **CLOTHES RACKS** in white or stained wood finish, personalized, *at right*

VdeB **DISPLAY STANDS**, plastic: small, medium, large, with signature logo on front, *at right*

VanderBear Family **DOOR STICKER & STORE SIGN**, *at right*, "Classic Velvet"

SPINNER DISPLAY, "Life is one big dress up" turnstile with easel back, *at right*

Muffy Rose

- Second Boxed Limited Edition of 10,000 for Club Members only
- Green satin body suit with rose petal sleeves and green ruffled collar
- Rose and green leaf petal taffeta over-skirt with a jeweled dew drop
- Gold ribbon rose trimmed slippers
- Flower pot hat with rose petals, ribbons, and a jeweled dew drop
- Gold personalized watering can
- Rose trellis display box with lattice-work doors and green ribbon tie
- Certificate of authenticity with Limited Edition number
- Factory Dressed only

Holiday Sticker Book

30 stickers from 6 retired holiday collections. *Sticker Book is pictured on page 28.*

Walking in Eggshells:
The Egg Painting Collection

Muffy: white eggshell cap and play suit with pastel stripe pattern, miniature color swatch card on wrist

Hoppy: similar to Muffy's outfit with lavender background, swatch card on wrist

Egg Decorating Kit: oval tin with 3 wax crayons, paper egg collars, sheet of water transfers, stencils, All-Natural Egg Recipe Dyeing Book, hangtag, tin is 6-1/2" x 4-1/2" x 1-3/4"

Egg Cups: Muffy and Hoppy in hand-painted porcelain, personalized, boxed, Muffy is 2-1/4" x 3-1/2" and Hoppy is 2-1/4" x 4"

Retired early because of difficulty with fabric.

Shown at left: Muffy and Hoppy with Egg Decorating Kit, Egg Cups, and Egg Painting Collectors Eggs. Collectors Eggs are described below.

Collectors Eggs

Hand-painted resin, inspired by old time sugar eggs, with Muffy and Hoppy posing in Easter Collections: *Muffy Bunny, Muffy Chick, Muffy Easter Fantasy, Hoppy Easter Fantasy, Muffy Egg Painting, Hoppy Egg Painting*, 3-1/2", boxed. (Muffy and Hoppy Egg Painting Collectors Eggs are *pictured above.*)

The Queen of Hearts and the Bunny Knave

The classic nursery rhyme for a Valentine's Day Tea.

Muffy: polished cotton gown of love notes and candy hearts with eyelet neck ruff, golden crown**, red French court shoes

Hoppy: ruffle collared knave costume, red slippers, peppermint swirl hat, and the joker card under her arm

Love Note Stationery Set: royal fabric chest with 12 embossed love notes, 12 envelopes, 3 sticker sheets, 4 colored pencils, hangtag, 6-1/4" x 4-1/4" x 3-1/2"

Rubber Stamp and Ink Pad: heart-shaped, featuring Muffy, with red ink pad, packaged with header, 2-1/2" x 2-1/4"

**Crown is attached on factory dressed bear.*

10th Anniversary
This Takes The Cake

- Boxed Limited Edition
- French blue taffeta gown with two-tiered scalloped skirt with golden swags, lace, pansies, yellow sash
- Black patent shoes with ribbon ties
- Crown of 10 "candles"
- Decorated gift box with certificate of authenticity on the side
- Factory Dressed only

> *Hangtag Note*
> *Round tag with pansy border. "Muffy VanderBear," "Tenth Anniversary" and "This Takes The Cake" are in purple and gold.*

Muffy Trivia
Muffy is 10 years old in people years; in bear years she is much younger. That way she never has to grow up!

Beauty is Only Fur Deep: The Boudoir Collection

Muffy: cream cotton pique robe with monogrammed pocket, quilted collar and cuffs, insignia ribbon tie; quilted satin beauty mask; fur-trimmed satin slippers

Muffy's Dressing Screen: hinged wooden screen with striped fabric inserts, personalized flower motif, 11-7/8" x 8-5/8" x 3/8"

Muffy's Vanity and Bench: wood with adjustable, personalized mirror, two drawers, matching bench with striped cushion, 9-1/8" x 10" x 3-1/2"

Muffy's Vanity Accessories: frosted glass powder jar with silvery lid and powder puff, silvery hand mirror and brush, frosted glass atomizer for Muffy's pretend perfume "Furissimo," with antiqued relief images of Muffy as a Grecian Muse, boxed, 10-1/4" x 2-1/4" x 5-3/4"

New Armoire Accessories

Hat Boxes: set of 3 (6-3/8", 5-1/2", and 4-3/8" in diameter) in pink custom print hat paper with VdeB ribbon handles

Hangers: 4 white plastic with pink Muffy cameo, 5", packaged with header

Garment and Shoe Bag Set: in custom print chintz, packaged with header, each is 7-1/2" long

Boot Box: custom boot print paper with 2 sliding compartments, 4-3/4" x 2" x 4-3/4"

Hat boxes were retired Spring 1997.

Clubhouse Collection:
What's The Secret Password?

Fuzzy: green carpenter's pants, beanie, suede sandals, T-shirt with "Dancing Hammer"

Muffy: periwinkle tie-on overalls with "Walking Clubhouse" logo, Jughead hat**, orange T-strap jelly sandals

Hoppy: yellow button rompers with "question mark", green T-strap jelly sandals, playhat

Muffy's Secret Clubhouse: wood grain cardboard with illustrations, boxed with instructions, assembled size is 15" x 10" x 8-1/2"

Clubhouse Accessories: wooden cigar box with secret treasures, contains list of rules inside cover, 2 decals, 40 original stamps, memo pad with logo, tin of 12 membership cards, 7" x 1-1/4" x 5"

**Hat is attached on factory dressed bear.

Muffy Trivia
Muffy master-minded the Clubhouse, Hoppy drew the plans, and Fuzzy built it. The secret password has never been revealed!

1994

Rose Frame

Third renewel gift for 4th year Club members: hand painted resin, Muffy tending the roses, 7-1/2" x 6-1/2". *Frame is pictured on page 126.*

Birthday Card II

From Muffy to Club members: Muffy "Flying Through". *Card is pictured on page 127.*

Tricky Treat Trio

Countess Muffula: paper mâché mask, cape, bat motif pants, "M" dickey, fuchsia bow tie

Hoppy Harecrow: striped trousers, plaid patched shirt, burlap stuffing, burlap hat with crow

Oatsie Oaterpillar: caterpillar costume

Tricky Treat Sticker Book: pumpkin-shape with 32 original stickers

Halloween Paper Decorations: set of 3, Muffy, Hoppy, & Oatsie, with springy pleated tissue arms and legs, each 12" long, packaged with header

Bathtime Collection
Splish Splash

Muffy: hooded turquoise terry cloth robe and bunny washmitt

Hoppy: hooded orange terry cloth robe and bear washmitt

Muffy's Bathtime Tub: porcelain, aquatic illustrations, gold fish feet, 9" x 4" x 6", boxed

Muffy's Bathtime Pitcher and Bowl: illustrated porcelain set, pitcher 2-1/2"x 2-3/4", boxed

Muffy's Bathtime Washstand: wooden, marbleized backsplash with bas-relief illustrations, 5-3/4" x 6"x 4", boxed

Muffy's Bathtime Towels: 1 terry towel, 6-5/8" x 9-7/8", with Muffy and Hoppy appliqué; 2 face towels, 3-1/2" x 5", with "H" and "M" monograms packaged with header

Hoppy, Washstand, and the Pitcher and Bowl were retired before the rest of the collection. Both Hoppy and the Pitcher and Bowl were sold out before dealer's reorders were filled.

1994   Travel Trunk

Classic steamer trunk with telescoping hanger racks, one drawer, and one shelf; interior with printed paper of Muffy on her travels; faux leather exterior, metal corners, travel stickers, 7" x 11-1/2" x 6-5/8"

1994   Figurines

Hand painted resin scenes, replicas of retired collections: **Day in the Country, Sailor, Gibearny, High Tea, Safari**, 2-3/4"x 2-3/4", boxed, shown at left

1994   Ornaments

Third group in series of resin holiday ornaments: **10th Anniversary, Alpine, Snowflake, Muffy of the North**, 2-1/2", boxed. *Ornaments are picture on page 55.*

1994   Gallery

Resin frames with printed reproductions of past collections, each holds a 3" x 5" picture, boxed: **Bal Masque, Musical Soirée, Nutcracker,** *shown above top right.*

1994   10th Anniversary Pin

Hand painted resin, 2-1/4" x 2", packaged. Muffy Anniversary head with purple banner: "Muffy 10th Anniversary".

1994   Retired Collection Tags

Special round hangtag indicates retired collections, gold with red border, Family tag is 2" diameter, Muffy/Hoppy tag is 1-1/2", *shown above top right.*

Muffy of the North

- Holiday Boxed Limited Edition
- "Fur" trimmed Eskimo parka with seal motif on cuffs and hem
- Sueded mukluks and mittens detailed with Inuit-inspired designs (Inuit is the Eskimo's name for themselves.)
- Pet white seal tied to right arm
- Illustrated igloo-shaped box with certificate of authenticity on the back
- Factory Dressed only

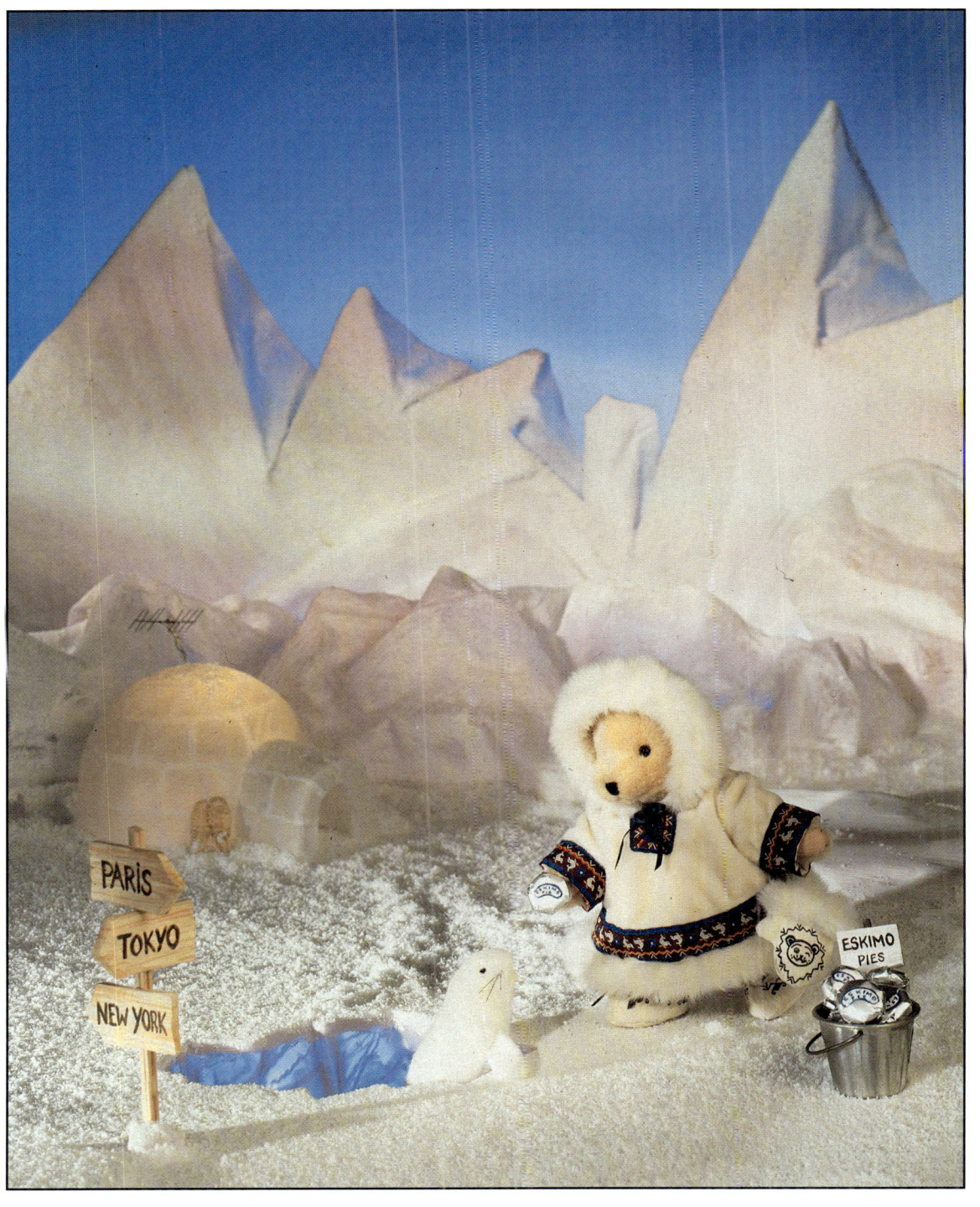

Hangtag Note
Blue and white tag with red border. "Muffy VanderBear" and "Muffy of the North" are printed in blue.

Muffy Trivia
Muffy's pet seal was named I.M. Chilly through a contest in Fanfare.

The North Pole Collection: Santa's Workshop

VanderBear Family Holiday trek to the North Pole to help Santa get ready for Christmas

Cornelius: Lapp-inspired folk costume, sueded boots, fleece hat, felt belt

Alice: folk dress with eyelet apron, tassel boots, traditional headdress

Fluffy: a baby doll in flowered corduroy dress, matching hat with felt wind-up key in back, white boots, paper baby doll mask

Fuzzy: sci-fi robot costume, square robot boots, antennaed helmet, paper mask

Muffy Santa: velveteen jacket, reindeer print pants, felt beard, plush trimmed hat, felt boots

Hoppy Elf: sueded lace-up jacket, polka dot pants, felt hat, striped socks, curled elf boots

Lulu Reindeer: antlers and harness

Muffy's North Pole Sled: natural wood, burned-in Lapp-land designs, medallion, ribbon lacing, 10" x 5" x 3-1/2"

Muffy's Sack of Toys: monogrammed felt bag with 4 embroidered toys inspired by Laplander folk art, 2-1/2" x 5" x 2-1/2", packaged with header

Muffy's Trim-A-Tree Kit: illustrated tin box that contains an 8" tree with wooden base, base cover, Muffy Santa tree topper, 12 original ornaments from the Collection with white ribbon, finished photograph, hangtag, tin box is 8-3/4" x 4-1/2" x 6-1/2"

Muffy's Water Ball: Muffy with Lulu and Sled, 3" x 4-1/2", boxed

Wrapping Paper: (30" x 20" sheets)
Reindeer Set with 2 sheets, 4 gift stickers, 2 paper ribbons, packaged
Muffy and Flower Set with 2 sheets, 4 gift cards, 2 paper ribbons, packaged

* Most pieces were still available into 1996, except for Muffy. Both factory dressed Muffy and Muffy outfit were sold out prior to their retirement announcement. North Pole was the first Lulu to retire.

Hangtag Note: Folded

Pajama Game

Fluffy: printed patchwork night dress with pink collar, monogrammed pocket, pink bear slippers

Fuzzy: patchwork pajamas with blue monogrammed pocket, blue bunny slippers

Muffy: striped pajamas, tasseled nightcap. pink bunny slippers, felt sheep on right wrist

Hoppy: checked pajama romper, blue bear slippers, felt and cotton kitten on left wrist

Muffy's Night-stand: wooden, monogrammed top, open shelf, 4" x 3-3/4" x 3-1/8", boxed

Muffy's Quilt: pieced patchwork, pink thread ties, 13-1/2" x 11-1/2", packaged with header & illustrated insert

Muffy's Lamp: monogrammed base with 5 tiny sheep, paper shade with cut-out stars, battery operated, 4-1/2" x 3-1/8", boxed

* Fluffy and Fuzzy were retired in Spring 1997, but Fuzzy was sold out before the end of 1996.

✽*Variation:*

Later Muffys had lighter pink slippers.

Fuzzy's slippers also came in different colors of blue.

The Mozart Collection: One Minuet More

Muffy Mozart: moiré frock coat, stripe vest, breeches, lace jabot, plastic wig, French court shoes

Hoppy Diva: 18th C. taffeta dress, "Hoppy" in musical notes on bodice, gold shoes, tricorn hat

Muffy Spinet: 18th Century reproduction, "M" music rest, musical - Mozart's Zubearflotte (The Magic Flute), bench with moiré cushion matching Muffy's coat, 7" x 5" x 4-1/2"

Muffy's Little Theatre: cardboard Rococo stage and props, die cut, to assemble, 13" x 12" x 8-1/4", boxed

> *Hangtag Note:*
> *Hoppy first issued with "VanderBear" hangtag, corrected later to "VanderHare".*

Birthday Card III

From Muffy to Club members: Muffy & Hoppy figures spelling Happy Birthday. *Card is pictured on page 127.*

Fan Shape Box

4th renewal gift for 5th year Club members: pink and gold porcelain, black tassel, gift boxed with a thank you note from Muffy, 4-3/4" x 2-1/2". *Frame is pictured on page 126.*

Princess Muffy and the Pea

- Third Boxed Limited Edition of 15,000 for Club Members only, storybook role
- Elegant cotton nightdress with empire bodice decorated with pea blossoms, ribbons, and lace
- Attached golden crown with "emeralds"
- Illustrated canopy bed to assemble with 5 floral print mattresses, a tiny green "pea" sewn to the bottom, ladder
- Certificate of Authenticity and Limited Edition number
- Factory Dressed only

Hangtag Note
Folded pea green tag with "Muffy VanderBear" in blue and "Princess Muffy and the Pea" printed in yellow. Story inside.

All Paws on Deck

1995-1999

VanderBear Family

Cornelius: cotton twill middy blouse, button-front sailor pants, sailor hat, espadrilles

Alice: twill middy dress with lace-up front and anchor buttons, straw sailor hat, espadrilles

Fluffy: old-fashioned bathing costume, plaid tie, "Float-A-Bear" waterwings

Muffy: twill middy dress with red trim, anchor buttons, plaid tie, embroidered collar, black espadrilles, treasure map rolled into plastic tube on wrist that can be folded into hat

Hoppy: middy dress with black trim, treasure map, red espadrilles

Lulu: life preserver with "All Paws On Deck" motto

Muffy's Boat, The Lulu: wooden dingy, vellum paper sail, "Muffy" painted on the side, 16" x 6" x 14"

> **Muffy Trivia**
> The adventure takes place on Cornelius' new Boat, Alice II

1995   Bags, Balloons, Folders, Postcards, Buttons

SHOPPING BAG, triangular **GIFT BAG** (with tissue and tag), **FOLDER**, 18" **SIGN**, **BALLOON**, new logo **POSTCARD**, and new logo **BUTTON**. *Most items are pictured on page 127.*

1995   Brochure

Muffy's "Amazing Armoire" paper fold-out brochure with photos of Muffy and her wardrobe and a history of the VanderBears. *Brochure is pictured on page 127.*

Checkmates

Muffy: lavender linen pinafore, acorn buttons, chess print bandanna, yellow flocked Mary Janes

Hoppy: orange linen pinafore, carrot buttons, chess print bandanna, blue flocked Mary Janes

Chess Set: modeled after all of Muffy and Hoppy's friends in decorative box with game board, 9" x 9", average chess piece is 1-5/8"

Checkmate Chairs: wooden bear chair, 7-1/2" x 5-1/2" x 4", and bunny chair, 9" x 5-1/2" x 4"

Checkmate Table: wooden, carrot and acorn designs and drawer pulls, 9" x 9" x 4-1/4"

Muffy Trivia
Hoppy's pawns are carrots, representing clarity of vision and thought. Muffy's pawns are acorns, symbolizing the strength of the mighty oak

Czarina Muffina

- Traditional Russian costume from the Imperial era
- Korotenka (pearl buttoned challis overdress)
- Sarafan (underdress)
- Rubacha (cotton blouse)
- Koko shnik (velveteen head dress), "Muffy" embroidered backward and forward with gold and pearls

- Gold trimmed black velveteen boots
- Black velboa swan with red neck bow that ties to Czarina's korotenka

> **Muffy Trivia**
> *Muffy and Hoppy's Magical Fairy Tale*
> When Muffy offers the black swan her carrot, and amazing transformation takes place. The swan becomes her true bunny self—Hoppy Hopponova, freed from an evil spirit.

Hangtag Note: Accordion folded

Sleddin' and Skidaddlin': A Winter Frolic

New England Holiday in Bearmont

Muffy: Norwegian cardigan, tasseled cap, corduroy knickers, lace-up ski boots

Hoppy: crewneck sweater, tasseled cap, corduroy knickers, lace-up ski boots

Lulu: sweater with tasseled hood, outfit packaged on cardboard cutout of Lulu

Skis and Poles: wooden, decorated with Norwegian rosemaling, 8-1/4" x 1-1/4" skis, 6" poles

Sled: wooden, decorated with rosemaling, 9-1/2" x 3-1/2" x 1-1/4"

Backpack, Scarf, and Mittens for Muffy and Hoppy: each set contains a corduroy backpack with buckle, scarf, and mittens; Muffy's set is in rose and Hoppy's set is in plum; each set packaged as outfits only on cardboard cutouts

> **Muffy Trivia**
> Muffy's Sled belonged to Cornelius when he was a cub.

Muffy Mouse

- Holiday Boxed Limited Edition
- Edwardian style suit with lace edged collar and cuffs, 2 yellow "cheesy" buttons at waist
- Whiskered rubber nose
- Pink tail with ribbon
- "Cheesy" lace-up slippers
- Personalized striped stocking
- Plate of cheese and crackers for Santa, dated 1995
- Illustrated book box inspired by the famous "Twas The Night Before Christmas" poem with certificate of authenticity on the back
- Factory Dressed only

Hangtag Note:
Round tag with Muffy Mouse pictured. "Muffy Mouse" and "1995 Limited Edition" are printed in yellow.

New England Country Christmas

VanderBear Family Holiday at their rustic farmhouse in Bearmont

Cornelius: herringbone vest and trousers, band collared shirt, stenciled hanky, red velvety slippers

Alice: red sweater with grosgrain bows and monogram, lace cuffs, pleated plaid skirt tied with bows

Fluffy: plaid drop waist jumper, muslin blouse with ruffled collar, red slippers, plaid head bow

Fuzzy: herringbone knickers with suspenders, muslin shirt, red slippers

Muffy: lace trimmed green gingham dress, muslin pinafore tied at shoulders, satin bows**, white felt boots, calico kitten (Purrlie) tied to her right sleeve

Hoppy: red gingham lace edged dress, muslin pinafore tied in back, felt boots, red and green ear bows

Lulu: stenciled muslin bib, yellow bow on her ear, outfit packaged on illustrated insert

Muffy's Hot Chocolate Set: 10 piece hand painted ceramic set, illustrated box

Muffy's Country Christmas Table: stained wood with original artwork, monogrammed, 11" x 8" x 5-3/4"

Muffy's Country Christmas Chairs: 2 monogrammed wooden chairs with gingham cushions, 4-1/2" x 3-1/2" x 7-1/2"

Muffy's Country Christmas Cookie Tin:* 7 plastic cookie cutters and recipe card, hangtag, in 4" x 2" tin

Cookie Tin sold out and retired in December 1995

**Bows are attached on factory dressed bear*

> **Hangtag Note:**
> Round tag in country colors. "Muffy VanderBear" is in red and "New England Country Christmas" is printed in green and red.

Paint The Town Red

A romantic Valentine night on the town, factory dressed only. Limited Numbered Edition of 4,500 each

Cornelius: red striped shirt, checked trousers, matching print bow tie and suspenders, two-tone spats, heart-shaped box of love tokens

Alice: red crushed velvet dress and cloche hat, monogrammed chiffon scarf, black handbag and shoes

Hangtag Note:
Blue, red, and purple background with paint brush. "Paint The Town Red" is printed in black and white, and Cornelius or Alice's name is in white.

Hearts and Flowers

- Cherry red & white dress with lace heart bodice and a printed cross-stitched border
- Cotton batiste hanky with lace edge and embroidery, attached to skirt
- Red Mary Janes
- Organza headbow** with forget-me-nots

**Bow is attached on factory dressed bear.

Hangtag Note:
Round tag with cross-stitched heart. "Muffy VanderBear" is in black and "Hearts and Flowers" is printed in blue and red.

Spring Bonnets:
The Silly Milly-nery Collection

Muffy, Hoppy, and Lulu make their own bonnets for the Easter Parade.

Muffy: drop-waist pink "hat print" dress with scalloped collar and spring bow, black patent Mary Janes, white socks, green felt up-side down bonnet with chick

Hoppy: green smock dress in "hat print" with eyelet collar, black patent Mary Janes, socks, red hat

Lulu: purple felt doggy bowl hat with bone

*Jewelry Tin: kit with 9 Easter Collection charms, 6 blue eggs, green & pink cord, assembly suggestions, hangtag, 5-3/4" x 2-1/2" x 3/4". Tin illustrated with charms on top and the words "Trinkets and charms — Muffy's springtime jewelry kit."

*The Jewelry Tin retired unexpectedly in April 1996.

> *Hangtag Note:*
> *Large tag with butterflies and flowers. "A Silly Milly-nery Collection" and "Spring Bonnets" are in green. "Muffy" is in red.*

Cocoa Bunny

Hoppy: In chocolate velour bunny suit with purple satin ear lining, and purple trim, *first Hoppy issued by herself*

Wheelbarrow: Hand-painted, rustic wood with "Choco Loco Motion" on one side, "M & H Eggspress" on the other, filled with excelsior, 8-1/4" x 4-1/8"

Hangtag Note Chocolate easter egg decorated with "Cocoa Bunny" in purple and "Hoppy VanderHare" in white.

The Reading Collection:
A to Z by M. V. deB.

Muffy in alphabet print dress with her name spelled in buttons around her waist, felt slippers, tortoise-shell glasses with a ribbon to go around her neck

ROCKER and CUSHION, cream wood with tied cushion, embroidered with "Muffy", 7-1/4" x 5-1/4" x 5-1/4"

Purrlie: is all grown up with plaid neck bow, 4"

Purrlie's **BASKET & CUSHION**, wicker, name embroidered on cushion, packaged with header, 5-1/4" x 3-1/4" x 1-1/4"

Hangtag Note
Muffy's coloring book: A to Z by McVdeB

Take A Hike:
A Walk On The Wylde Side

Cornelius: barn jacket with "Take a Hike Society" patch, plaid shorts, moccasins

Alice: blue smock with red buttons, blue tam, moccasins

Fluffy: pink-print smock and tam, moccasins

Fuzzy: barn jacket with Society patch, plaid shorts, moccasins

Muffy: feather-print jacket with monogrammed snaps, Society patch, plaid shorts, ear-flapped hat, moccasins

Hoppy: gold thistle-print jacket with pewter snaps and Society patch, plaid shorts, hiking hat, moccasins

Bench: rustic wood with Society plaque, 11" x 6" x 3-1/4"

**Family retired 1999.
Muffy, Hoppy and
Wooden Bench retired
2001.*

*Hangtag Note
"Muffy's
Sketchbook" is a 4
page tag bound with
twine. It hangs
around her neck, not
on her waist as stat-
ed in the catalog.
Hoppy's tag is
a journal.*

1996   **MUFFY VANDERBEAR CLUB KIT II** with new stickers, new stationery, and new Collection Album

MUFFY STATIONERY & STICKERS, with Muffy Butterfly and Rose: 10 sheets & envelopes, 1 sheet of stickers, for Club members only. *Both are pictured on page 127.*

COLLECTION ALBUM for new and renewing Club members: 2 ring, hard linen covered binder with new ribbon logo on the cover and picture inserts that will be updated, 8" x 8" x 2". *Album is pictured on page 127.*

Muffy Pierrot
First Collector's Edition

- Limited Edition of 20,000*
- White velvet suit with black pompons and black trimmed ruffled collar
- Black satin hat and black satin slippers
- Mime mask on beribboned stick
- Marionette Pierrette bunny
- French puppet theater box, with certificate of authenticity on the back
- Factory dressed only

Hangtag Note
Vertical tag with Pierrot pictured. "Muffy Pierrot" and "Collector's Edition" are printed on the front.

First numbered limited edition available to non-club members, number is written on tag sewn onto bare Muffy. Sewn in labels mistakenly printed with club reference. See page 134.

Happy Birthday To YOU

Muffy: pastel taffeta check dress with lace-edged sleeves, petticoat, pink ribbon sash, pale pink Mary Janes, matching bow**, rolled party favor crown on her wrist, and a special card to send in and receive a gift from Muffy — a *Happy Birthday Magnet*!

Hoppy: pastel striped taffeta dress with lace-edged collar, petticoat, pale green Mary Janes, matching bow, party favor hat on her wrist, and a special card to send in and receive a gift from Muffy

Lulu: eyelet collar matching Muffy's petticoat, rolled party hat, outfit packaged with header

Oatsie: blue felt "Pin the Tail on the Donkey" costume, outfit packaged on cutout

Birthday Party Set: 4 decorated 2-1/4" plates, 3-1/8" cake stand, 4 monogrammed 2-3/4" spoons in birthday check box

Tablecloth and Seat Cushions: 12" x 16" cloth and 2 taffeta tie-back cushions to fit the New England Country Christmas Table and Chairs and 1997 Portrait Table and Chairs, packaging contains a birthday banner and placecards, packaged with header

Cake: resin, decorated in pink with "Happy Birthday To You," 1-1/2" x 2-1/2", boxed

**Bow is attached on factory dressed bears.

Hangtag Note
Oval tag with pastel check border and a birthday cake in the middle. "Muffy VanderBear" is in green and "Happy Birthday To You" is printed in blue.

Club T-Shirt

2 designs: (1) 5 lavender ribbon logo Muffys with "Muffy Club Charter Member Founded 1990" underneath, for charter members only and (2) a larger single Muffy Club ribbon logo for all Club members

---

Birthday Card IV

From Muffy to Club members: Birthday Cake. *Card is pictured on page 127.*

Cheerleading:
Go...Go...Go Fur It!

Muffy: red corduroy skirt, white varsity cardigan sweater with "M", plaid bodysuit with white collar trimmed in red, headbow** with "Go Bears, Go Hares, Go Pups," saddle shoes

Hoppy: blue corduroy skirt, plaid bloomers, varsity V-neck sweater with "H", headbow and saddle shoes

Lulu Mascot: hooded sweater, outfit packaged on Lulu cutout

Accessories: felt pennant, megaphone, ribbon pompons, boxed with 4 cut-out trading cards on the back

**Bow is attached on factory dressed bear.

Hangtag Note Oval with red border. "Go...Go...Go Fur It!" is printed in red, yellow, and blue. "Cheerleading" and "Muffy VanderBear" is in blue.

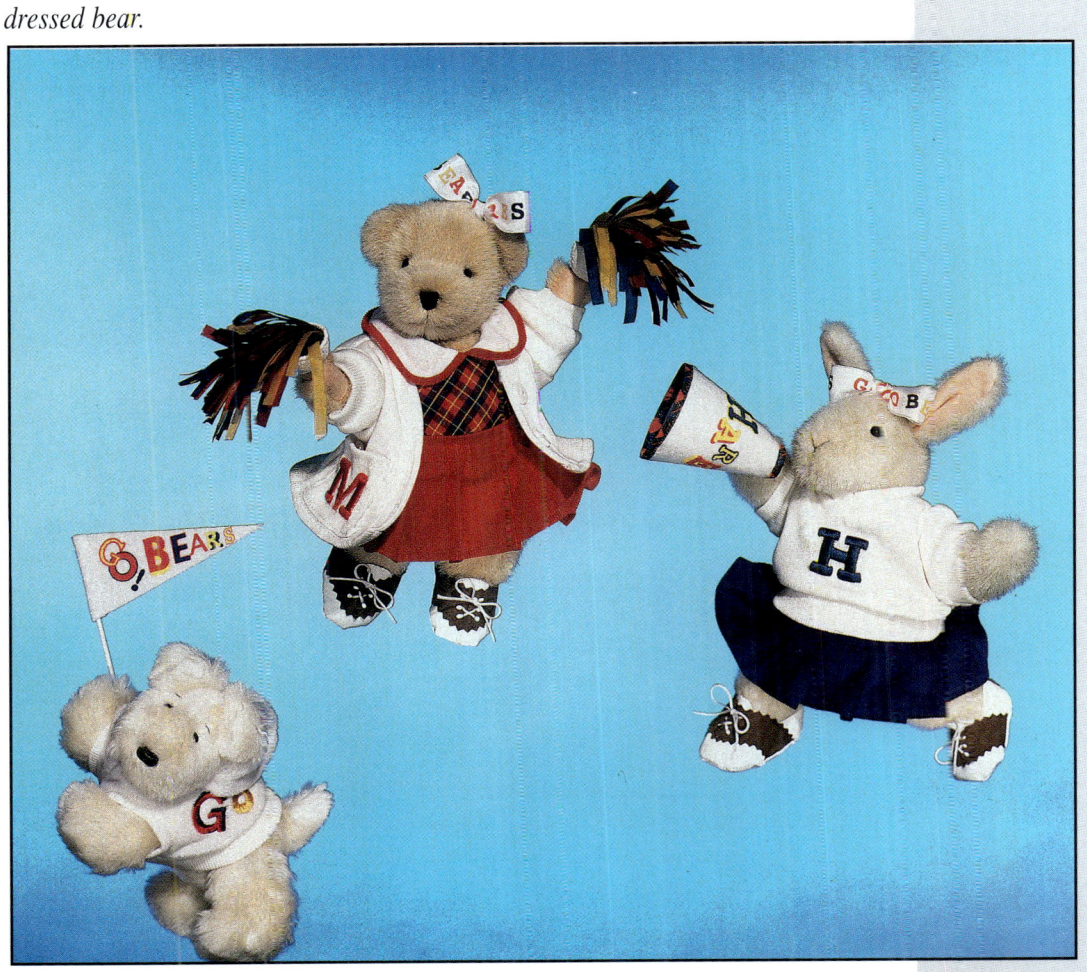

Bare Muffy Hangtag

1996

New folded hangtag with blue border was issued for undressed Muffys in Fall 1996

Lulu

1996

New oval hangtag with a border of bones, but same *Highland Fling* plaid bow

1996-1996

Muffy The Red-Nosed ReinBear

- Holiday Boxed Limited Edition
- Brown Jumpsuit
- Separate hood with ears, antlers, and Rudolf-red pompon nose
- Mittens embroidered with "M" and Hoof slippers embroidered with holly motifs
- Decorated green felt goodie bag around her neck with a Santa doll inside
- Illustrated house box, with certificate of authenticity on the back
- Factory dressed only

1996

Sleepshirt & T-Shirt

SLEEPSHIRT for adults with Muffy *Pajama Game* on the front, one size. **T-SHIRT** with single Muffy lavender ribbon logo, but without the words Club or Charter Member like the Club shirts described on *page 88*, available in adult and children's sizes

1996

Muffy Mailer

Promotional brochure featuring current Muffy Collections, 6 page fold-out, 7-3/4" x 10-7/8"

A Christmas Carol: Bearly In Tune

VanderBear Family Holiday, Christmas Caroling

Cornelius: woolly plaid double breasted coat with velvet collar, cuffs, covered buttons and pocket flaps; trousers to match; red satin ascot; spat boots; Hambearg style bowler

Alice: embroidered green velvet hooded cape trimmed in white "fur" and tied with checked ribbon, red satin underdress trimmed with white lace and ribbon at the neck, dark green sueded boots

Fluffy: velvet dress coat trimmed at collar and hem with white "fur", velvet hat, green sueded spat boots

Fuzzy: woolly plaid suit and cap with velvet collar, buttons, and pocket flaps; dark green velvet knickers; sueded shoes

Muffy: dark green embroidered velvet hooded cape trimmed with white "fur" and plaid bow, red satin underdress trimmed with white lace and ribbon, burgundy sueded spat boots with white trim and green buttons

Hoppy: velvet coat trimmed with white "fur" and embroidered capelet, embroidered velvet hat with plaid bow, sueded spat boots

Lulu: green velvet cape lined with red satin and ribboned tophat

Oatsie: embroidered woolly plaid horse blanket lined in satin, ribbon harness & blinders

Muff and Reticule: white "fur" muff with satin lining and cord, red embroidered bag with white tassel, packaged as a set in illustrated box

Landau: 18th century four-wheeled horse drawn carriage with raised seat for driver, working doors, bench seat, canopy that opens and closes, decorated with gold scrolling and "VdB" family crest, 22" x 12" x 8-3/4"

Lantern: "antique" embossed metal with bas reliefs of Muffy, Hoppy, and Lulu, batteries included, box is illustrated 1-5/8" x 1-5/8" x 3"

The Christmas Carol Family members (Cornelius, Alice, Fluffy, and Fuzzy) were retired by North American Bear Co. in Spring 1997 but stock ran out Fall of 1996. Stores received their first orders and were able to reorder a small number of pieces until available stock was gone. Landau retired and sold out Spring 1997. Oatsie retired Fall 1997.

Variation: Oatsie's outfit later changed to green velvet.

Hangtag Note
Folded songbook tag with title: ***A Christmas Carol***
Barely In Tune; SUNG BY Muffy VanderBear

The Messenger of Love

Hoppy: candy-striped overalls with embroidered scooter on the bib, blue high-top sneakers with embroidered hearts, messenger's cap, a blank letter (to be delivered to the Valentine of your choice) tucked inside her logo mail pouch, heart shaped hangtag

Scooter: red wooden "Hare-ly Davidson" scooter with carrot handle grips and hangtag

---

Trivia:
Hoppy wore her messenger outfit for the first Hoppy Events in 1998.

1997-1999*

A Salad Ballad: Waltz of the Vegetables

Fluffy - the Gardener: veggie print jumper with plush eggplant and carrot peaking out of the pocket, canvas gardening glove, canvas hat, woven tote bag

Muffy - Queen of the Eggplants: velvety eggplant costume with organza skirt, felt hat** with organza bow and ladybug embroidery, sueded dance shoes** with ribbon laces

Hoppy - An Extra Ear-ly Carrot: velvety carrot bodice with organza skirt, felt shoes with ribbon laces, felt leaf-trimmed carrot hat with organza bow

Lulu - A Lulu of a Tomato: velour tomato-red jumpsuit with stem adornment and felt hat, outfit packaged on cutout

Purrlie - Purrfect Sweet Pea: velvety peapod suit with pompon peas and stem, outfit packaged on cutout

Watering Can and Gardening Tools: resin eggplant rake and carrot spade, white tin watering can with vegetable decal, in gift box printed with cut-out "seed packets"

Muffy's Apron & Tote Bag: veggie print, packaged with header on cutout

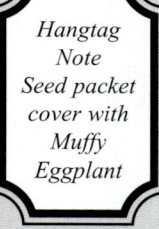

Hangtag Note Seed packet cover with Muffy Eggplant

Benchbarrow: green wooden wheel-barrow-shaped bench with Muffy and Hoppy cut-outs

Grown-up Tote Bag: canvas veggie pattern with "seed packet" pockets, 15" x 11" x 4", packaged with label

Grown-up Apron: cotton veggie pattern with "seed packet" pockets, packaged with label

*Grown-up apron and tote bag still available.

**Hat and shoes are attached on factory dressed bears

Square Dancing: Skip to My Lulu

Muffy: blue polkadot ric-rac trimmed bodysuit, tiered custom bandanna-print skirt with scalloped lace edging, red checked headbow**, little black flats

Hoppy: red checked buttoned-trimmed bodysuit with collar, tiered custom bandanna-print skirt with scalloped lace edging, red checked headbow, black flats

Lulu: tiered circle skirt and custom print bandanna

Patti: tie-back bandanna print vest, sueded boots (one pair)

Square Dancing Accessories: "Skip to My Lulu" print bandanna, straw hat with red checked tie, and sueded boots to fit Muffy, Hoppy, or Patti, packaged with header

*Muffy & Hoppy wear bodysuits, not blouses as stated in catalog.

**Headbow is attached on factory dressed bear.

> *Hangtag Note*
> *Country check print tag with "Square Dancing" and "Skip to My Lulu" at the top. "Muffy VanderBear" is printed across the bottom.*

E.R., O.R. & R n' R: Mercy Me Hospital

Head Nurse Muffy: white pique cotton uniform with navy silk-screened hospital logo on the pocket and sleeve, stylish nurse's cap, white plastic shoes.

Top Doc Hoppy M.D. x.y.z.: cotton scrubs with navy silk-screened hospital logo on the back and on the pocket, green cotton surgical cap, white mask; operating room clogs.

Lulu-Sick Pup: white hospital gown with a navy silk-screened hospital logo; removable cast (signed by pals) for her paw.

Doctor's Bag: complete with eight bandage stickers, pretend gauze bandages, instructions on bandaging, and three lollipops in illustrated box.

Ambulance (*not shown*) **& Stretcher** (**shown**): painted wooden ambulance with handle and hangtag, detachable stretcher with Lulu outline.

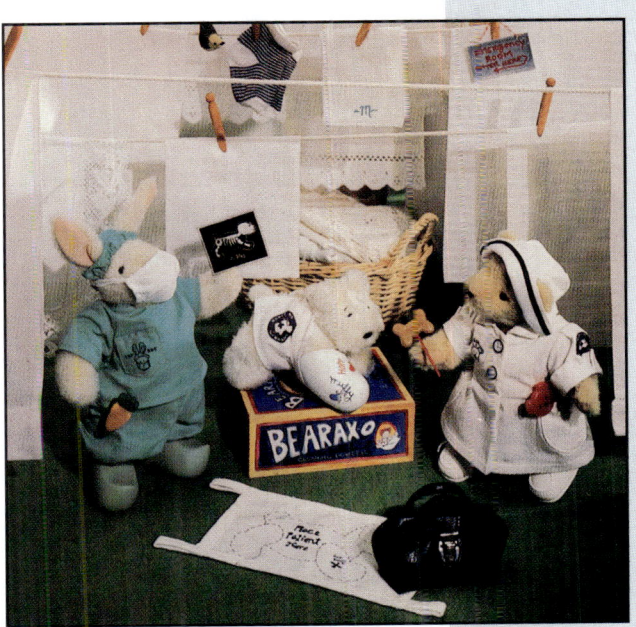

> *Hangtag Note*
> *Plastic hospital photo ID card.*

Abra-CadaBeara: Hoppus Poke-Us

1997-1997

The Great Hoppus Poke-Us makes a special appearance in her first Collector's Editon of 10,000 individually numbered pieces. She arrives in her caravan, a collectible box complete with certificate of authenticity.

Hoppus Poke-Us: cloak is a satin cape with black tux underneath; tuxedo shirt and oxford vest with silkscreened pattern of red and black cards; spats, matching wand and endless trick scarf. Out of her hat, Hoppy pulls a miniatured Muffionette wearing red dress and net cape with little hearts. Comes boxed in Hoppy's old world, gypsy-styled caravan.
Factory dressed only.
Hoppy's LE number is on the bottom of her foot.

Hangtag Note
"Hoppy's Book of Tricks."

Portrait Table & Chairs, Sitting Pretty

1997

Wooden table and 2 chairs with Muffy & Hoppy cutouts, same size as the New England Table & Chairs from 1995

Birthday Card V

1997-1997

From Muffy to club members: Muffy Happy Birthday pop-out

Muffy Pouch

1997

Renewal gift for club members, 5" x 7" plush zippered bag with coin purse and purple ribbon

Puttering Around

1997- 1997

Cornelius and Alice appear in a Numbered Limited Edition of 3,500 sets. They come boxed together, each with an individually numbered paw pad ribbon.

Alice: twill pleated skirt, red sweater with golfing bear motif, twill hat and red satin polka-dotted ribbon; brown and white golf shoes.

Cornelius: ivory twill knickers, red shirt, argyle knit seater vest with embroidered VdeB monogram; houndstooth check golfing cap; brown and white golf shoes; white canvas designer golf bag initialed with VB logo, a golf ball and tee, and three golf clubs.

Hangtag Note Double tags in the shapes of greens.

The Lemonade Stand: 5¢ a Glass

Muffy: pink pique pinafore that closes in back with a flower shaped button, lemon slice pockets; white pleated satin hat** with lemon floral trim; shoes—lemon yellow jellies

Hoppy: yellow trimmed tart green sundress; white pleated satin hat with lemon floral trim; shoes—lemon yellow jellies

Purrlie: wears a Sourpuss Café sandwich board; pink pique soda-jerk hat with lemon floral trim, factory dressed only

Lemonade Stand & Paper Aprons: Sourpuss Café lemonade stand, famous recipes featured on back; pad of twelve paper aprons and two ribbons, packaged with header, 8" x 10"

Pitcher and Glasses: frosted pitcher and set of four glasses with The Sourpuss Café logo in illustrated box

**Hat is attached on factory dressed bear

> *Hangtag Note*
> *Folded lemon-shaped tag. Inside: "Muffy*
> *was here" and "Service with a smile!"*

Muffy in WonBearLand

Displayed on top of a custom made Storybook

Cornelius as Mad Hatter: red wool jacket and over sized top hat

Alice as Queen of Hearts: hand-embroidered heart-strewn silk gown and jeweled crown

Muffy as Alice: silk taffeta outfit

Hoppy as White Rabbit: silk taffeta outfit

Lulu as Caterpillar: yellow and green striped suit

Purrlie as Cheshire Cat: cat mask

Fuzzy and Fluffy as Tweddle-Dee and Tweedle Dum: twin blue and white and red and white striped shirts with white button front pants

One-of-a-kind for Disney Convention Auction

Candy C'angel

Holiday Boxed Limited Edition

Muffy: red and white striped taffeta dress with matching candy-like button, ribbon collar, white taffeta pantaloons with red and white ric-rac trim, green grosgrain ribbon

Hangtag Note
Folded white, cloud-shaped tag with candy cane, "Candy C'angel" name and the words "Limited Edition"

Scared Stiff: The Foolish Ghoulish Collection

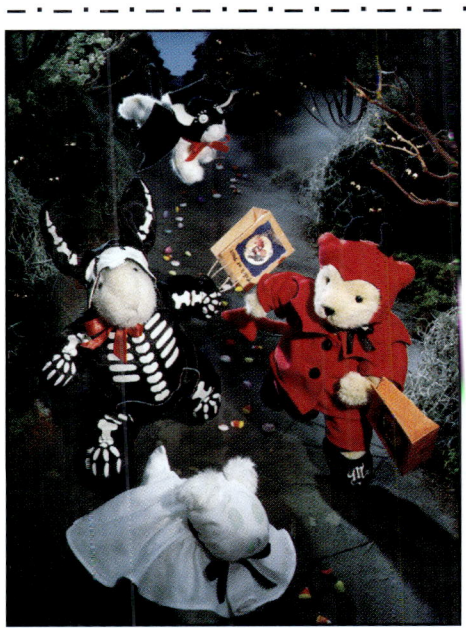

Muffy: red devil suit with tail and horns, glow-in-the-dark M's on black satin shoes, illustrated paper trick-or-treat bag

Hoppy: glow-in-the-dark bones on black satin jump suit, paper trick-or-treat bag

Lulu: white ghost outfit, glow-in-the-dark eyes, nose, and "Eeek, Boo and Screech" around hem

Purrlie: black hooded bat costume, velvety wings, glow-in-the-dark eyes

Foolish Ghoulish T-shirts

Hangtag Note Round folded tag in blue and orange identifies "Devil-May-Care" Muffy and pictures a tiny Purrlie Bat-Cat

Glass Ornaments

Featuring Muffy from boxed editions of Christmas past and present: Muffy of the North, Muffy Reinbear, Muffy Mouse and Candy C'angel

Muffy Peddler Doll

Muffy Peddler was an LE of 5000 For 1997 Walt Disney Teddy Bear & Doll Convention. Each **Muffy Peddler** is hand-numbered on the tag attached to her back. Dressed as a 19th century Peddler doll, Muffy bears tokens of each of the "Twelve Days of Christmas" with the lyrics of the famous song running around the hem of her dress. Her illustrated box resembles a peddler's stall. Factory dressed only

Hangtag Note Folded scroll-shaped tag tied to box with "parchment" insert explaining the history of Peddler dolls, includes the signatures of all 3 designers

---

Location of "The Twelve Days Of Christmas" Tokens on Muffy:

1. Partridge In A Pear Tree - embroidered on front of hat
2. Turtle Doves - shoes
3. French Hens - in left pocket
4. Calling Birds - embroidered on back of hat
5. Golden Rings - attached to wreath on tie around neck
6. Geese Laying - in carrying basket
7. Swans Swimming - paper cutouts in right pocket
8. Maids Milking - cow charm attached to apron
9. Ladies Dancing - charm attached to apron
10. Lords Leaping - charm attached to apron
11. Pipers Piping - charm attached to apron
12. Drummers Drumming - charm attached to apron

Muffy The Little MerBear

Fourth Boxed Club Edition

Hangtag Note Folded hangtag in sea blue with Muffy MerBear swimming in the sea and the words "Muffy The Little MerBear"

- Seafoam green velvet mermaid suit, embossed scallop pattern, pink, shellshaped bodice trimmed in pearls, tailfin embroidered with pearls forming a scrolling "M"
- Golden locks adorned with cast coral and pearl crown, pearlized shell-shaped compact, miniature Purrlie catfish
- Available exclusively to members of the Muffy VanderBear Club in a Limited Edition of 15,000
- Factory dressed only
- Muffy MerBear's Certificate of Authenticity is hand embossed with NABCO's designer seal which includes the initials of the Muffy design team: Barbara Isenberg, Odl Bauer, and Katya Bauer.

Muffy Tree Topper

Red taffeta gown printed with gold stars, pair of golden angel wings, wire-edge ribbon that says "Peace on Earth...Love Muffy"; golden halo of shimmering stars

Paris Bistrot: Le Lapin Rotund

Muffy: French red and white sailor shirt, blue skirt, high heels; wears beret** and carries concertina; bandanna around neck is printed with map of Paris

Hoppy: white chef's jacket, black and white houndstooth chef's pants, black Mary Janes; chef's hat embroidered with Lapin Rotund name

Lulu, Lulu Ze Poodle: poodlesque pom-poms, poodle jumpsuit, pink ribbon around neck

Bistrot Food Set with Apron & Tablecloth: baguette, bottle of vintage "*bear*jolais," blue and white checked tablecloth, chef apron, wheel of "Camembear" cheese

Hangtag Note Folded tag in blue and green identifies Muffy as 'Ze Cabearet Singer"

Bistrot Table & Chairs with Menu Board: white enameled metal table and chairs

Bistrot Lapin Rotund: painted backdrop, 12-1/2" x 11-1/2" x 6-7/8"

**Beret is attached on factory dressed bear.

A Legendary Family: Portrait in Black & White

Cornelius: quilted smoking jacket with embroidered pocket, plaid piping, frog closure, wears a white dickey with plaid bow tie black velvet pants and slippers, black velvet fez with tassle

Alice: white voile lace-trimmed blouse, bear cameo, long black velvet skirt, black and white T-Strap shoes, plaid taffeta headbow

Fuzzy: black velvet jacket and breeches, black and white braid trim, white shirt with lace detailed collar and cuffs and boasts a spiffy black and white plaid bow tie, side-snapped sueded boots

Fluffy: black and white plaid taffeta party dress with embroidered voile collar and black satin headbow, sueded party shoes that tie in front with satin bow

Muffy: black velvet dress with embroidered voile collar and ribbon-and-rose trim, black and white ribbon head bow, plaid taffeta pantaloons, sueded Mary Janes, sueded black and white taffeta purse stitched with her portrait

Hoppy: black velvet buttoned-front dress with embroidered ruffled collar, black and white plaid headbow, black and white plaid pantaloons, sueded Mary Janes, black purse stitched with her portrait

Lulu: black velvet quilted embroidered coat and hat

Purrlie: hooded black velvet coat with lace trim and embroidery

Piano Musicbox: black, 7" x 5" x 4-1/2"

Muffy and Hoppy's Pinafore and Headband: lace-trimmed black and white plaid taffeta pinafore that ties at the sides, black velvet headband topped off with bow

*VanderBear Family Display Sofa: Chippendale style sofa in white cotton twill with black buttons and taffeta trim. 33" x 20" x 19"

Portrait In Black & White Gifts, each is packaged with an illustrated gift box and tissue paper

*VanderFans Bearmés Scarf: with family crest, silk, 34" x 34"

*Cornelius's Boxer Shorts: cotton Santa-Bear print

*Alice's Bearmés Scarf: silk, featuring family crest and portraits, 16" x 16"

*Fluffy's Chemisette: cotton Santa-Bear print

*Fuzzy's Boxer Shorts: cotton Santa-Bear print

*Muffy's Bearmés Scarf: silk, featuring portraits of the family, 10" x 10"

*Hoppy's Earwarmers: knitted in orange carrot-shapes

*Lulu's Bedcover: cotton Santa-Bear print

*Purrlie's Bedcover: cotton Santa-Bear print

*Sofa and Portrait Gifts are retired.

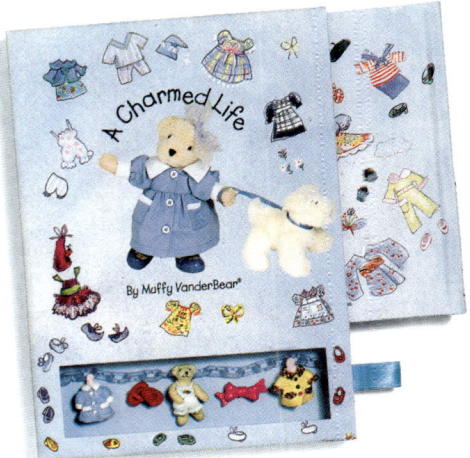

A Charmed Life

Full-color book with
photos and illustrations, packed with
charm bracelet with five plastic charms

Stroke-of-Midnight

Muffy, Cinbearella: jeweled crown, pink satin gown, glass slippers

Hoppy, Hare-y Godmother: silk organza wings, silk taffeta gown with ribbon ruffling, jeweled crown, glass carrot wand

Lulu, Coachpup: silk waistcoat and jabot, brocade vest, tritone hat

Purrlie, Slipper Bearer: feathered silk velvet page hat and brocade cape

Oatsie: silk brocade blanket with antique French ribbon trim, silk turban with feathers

Handmade wooden coach with gold trim, velvet interior, cushioned pumpkin top.

One-of-a-kind for Disney Convention Auction

Travel Trunk Clock

Club Renewal Gift: clock built into travel trunk with drawers, paper cutout clothes

---

Travel Trunk Set

• Durable steamer trunk, Muffy wearing Picking Posies dress
• Includes Happy Birthday to YOU!, Blue Pagoda, and Reading outfits

---

Bedroom Set

Armoire, Hangers, Bed, Bedding Accessories, Nightstand, and Dressed Muffy Pajama Game. After Muffy Pajama Game sold out - Muffy Sleepover was included.

Abearicana
Stars and Stripes Furever

Muffy: red, white and blue dress covered with stars and stripes, muslin work apron to embroider, a lace trimmed "mob" cap, and black buckled shoes

Hoppy: tricorn hat with a be-ribboned braid, a waistcoat, pot-bellied breeches, lantern, buckled shoes, and a "jabot" printed with stars and ready to embroider

Oatsie: star-printed muslin saddle to embroider, leatherette harness and bridle

Ladder-back Chair: wooden, 7-1/2" x 4-1/2" x 3-1/2"

Muffy's Embroidery Basket with Cushion Kit: fabric and wicker, wooden embroidery hoop and portrait cushion kit for ladder-back chair

Hangtag Note
Folded tag in shades of blue with teacup border and name of Collection

The Blue Pagoda:
All the Tea in China

Muffy: Princess "Muf-Fi" in blue and white print cotton tunic, matching cotton pants, print shoes, fabric headbow**, *Blue Pagoda* "tea bag" on wrist

Hoppy: Princess "Ho-Pi" in long printed polished cotton blouse joined with ribbons and buttons, traditionally styled pants, print shoes, headbow printed with "cup and saucer" coordinate, *Blue Pagoda* "tea bag" on wrist

Lulu: hat printed with story of tea pattern, with yellow tassel

Purrlie: Chinese beanie with long braid

Tea Set: porcelain teapot, four cups, four saucers, sugar bowl, creamer and tray, with *Blue Pagoda* pattern

Tea Time Linen Set: set of two cushions, tea cozy, four napkins

Blue Pagoda: pagoda topped with tea cups, decorated with illustrated tiles, cardboard sides unfold like Chinese screen, 13-3/4"W x 15-3/4"H x 4"D. Tea Table 5-1/4"W x 2-3/4"H

**Headbow is attached on factory dressed bear.

Grand VanderBall, A FunRaising Gala

Hangtag Note Folded white tag with plaid die-cut rosette in the corner includes Collection name

Cornelius, red-lapelled plaid taffeta dinner jacket, plaid rose boutonnière, piqué dickey with emerald studs, plaid bow tie, red taffeta pants, and black shoes

Alice: festive red taffeta ball gown, rouched sleeves, plaid rose, velvet leaf trim, embroidered details, bejewelled ear-bows, ribbon-tied black dancing slippers

Fuzzy: red lapelled plaid dinner jacket, boutonnière, piqué dickey, plaid bow, red pants, black shoes

Fluffy: tiered taffeta dancing gown trrimmed with a plaid rose and velvet leaves, plaid under-skirt, bejewelled headbow, ribbon-tied dancing slippers

Muffy: red taffeta ballgown with puffed sleeves and embroidered details, green satin sash trimmed with VanderBall motif, plaid rose and velvet leaf, plaid headbow**, formal white gloves, black dancing slippers with black bows

Hoppy: sleeveless decolletée ballgown of red taffeta with leaf embroidery, green satin sash trimmed with plaid rose and velvet leaf, plaid headbow, formal white gloves, black dancing slippers with bows

Lulu: black tuxedo jacket with white collar and black bow tie, silver "boutré" with doggie bonbons

Purrlie: maid headpiece and lace-trimmed white apron

GingerBear Manor Covered Box: resin, with removable lid, 3-1/2" x 3-1/4" x 2-1/2". Dessert Tray decorated with VanderBall rose motif, handles fashioned after Lulu and Purrlie, 4-1/2" x 2-3/4"

Taffeta Table-Runner and Chair Covers: Embroidered with VanderBall rose and leaf motif, red taffeta on one side, plaid on other, decorative tassels on either end, 19" x 6". Chair Covers embroidered "M" and "H," red taffeta, tie with plaid ribbons

Punch Bowl and Cups: clear acrylic, scalloped edge and frosted roses, four matching cups

Tiara and Necklace Set: silver with faux diamonds and emeralds, exclusively designed to fit either Muffy or Hoppy

**Headbow is attached on factory dressed bear.

Sweets for the Sweet

Muffy: belted vanilla corduroy jumpsuit with candy button and printed patch with Muffy's candy factory insignia on front, head bow** printed with dancing bonbons, frosty pink Mary Janes, regulation "fur-net"

Hoppy: "icing pink" corduroy jumpsuit with printed patch, two candy buttons, dancing bonbon headbow, ivory Mary Janes. "hare net"

Lulu: folding sample tray hanging around neck, felt bonbon hat with organza ruffle

Rudy: bright red cotton overalls with printed patch, candy buttons and red delivery cap

Delivery Cart: painted wood, candy wheel, hinged lid with candy knob; 3 bonbon mold trays, recipe booklet, and 6 candy bags with stickers. Size is 5-3/4"L x 4" H x 2-1/2"W

**Headbow is attached on factory dressed bear.

Hangtag Note
A flattened candy box in pink and cream that you can fill with your favorite candy, includes Collection name

---

Little BearPeep Collector's Edition

18th century Shepherdess dress with "polonaise" ribbon treatment, crisscrossed bodice with lace cuffs, underskirt of violet and white striped taffeta. Floral ribboned slippers, little pearl earrings, classic period cap topped by straw bonnet with floral bouquet. Staff with sheep charm. Mary wears a straw hat decorated with flowers and a plaid ribbon, four yellow felt shoes, sign that says "Lost" on one side, "Found" on the other. Comes in illustrated woods box with certificate of authenticity. Limited Boxed Edition of 15,000. Factory Dressed Only

Hangtag Note
Folded scalloped tag with Collection name, the words "Collector's Edition," and a funny lamb

Muffy Plum Fairy

Holiday Boxed Limited Edition
Layered purple tulle overskirt, plum colored, heart-shaped velvet bodice with shirred tulle sleeves. Underskirt of lavender taffeta printed with glittering plums, ribbons, and leaves. Velvety plum and flower crown, ballet slippers tied with ribbons, basket with resin sugar plums and miniature nutcracker.
Factory Dressed Only
Illustrated stage box

Hangtag Note
Folded Plum-shaped tag with the words "Muffy Plum Fairy"

1998

Spring Chickens

Hangtag Note Folded scalloped tag in blue & yellow with Collection name and picture of baby chick

Muffy: gingham checked voile pinafore with bloomers and pink Mary Janes, gingham checked hat with flower detail, white piqué apron with chick, flower and egg embroidery; pet chick in decorated egg, wicker stroller tied with ribbon to Muffy's wrist

Old Fashioned Paper Egg: cut paper design of Muffy with little chicks and eggs, filled with crinkly crepe paper, 5"

Picking Posies, Mum's the Word

Alice: blue custom print dress strewn with flowers, trimmed in lace, closes at back with "bear face" flower buttons, matching fabric shoes, organza headbow ribbon with hand-crocheted flowers

Muffy: spring green dress printed with bouquets of flowers, blue hand-crocheted sweater with green trim and flower closure, fabric headbow with hand-crocheted flower, floral print shoes

Lulu: fabric apron matching Muffy's dress, hand-crocheted blue hat with green trim

Muffy's Pick-a-Posy Set: pitcher-shaped vase, printed to match Muffy's dress, comes with Muffy-sized flower basket and paper flowers

Pin and Earring Gift Set: miniature "tussy-mussie" pin molded in shape of Muffy to hold together small bouquet of flowers, pierced earrings, cast with portraits of Muffy framed in posy petals

Hangtag Note
Folded round tag in spring green with Muffy head in center flower, includes Collection name

---

Play Date: A Toy Collection

Muffy: plaid romper with toy print fabric and coordinating plaid collar and cuffs, button on apron, felt-trimmed plaid shoes, two satin ear-bows, pocket with matching felt bear handpuppet

Hoppy: plaid romper with toy print collar, button-on apron, felt-trimmed print shoes, two satin ear-bows, pocket with matching bunny handpuppet

Muffy's Toy Chest with Puppet Theater and Toy Set: play date theme screened on top and sides, label on inside for personalizing wooden chest; 3 stacking paper blocks, carrot handled jump rope, rubber ball, collapsible puppet theater

Hangtag Note
Round folded tag in pink with jump-rope border and Collection name

1998

PocaHoppy

Hoppy: sueded fringed dress, traditional stitching on collar, sleeves and hem; fancy-stitched moccasins, headband of felt feathers, wampum bag with three paper bunny coins

1998

Signature Collection

Muffy: French blue cotton "signature print" dress with white portrait collar, French blue organza headbow**, darker blue Mary Janes

Muffy's Signature Knapsack, Stamp, Inkpad, and Notepad: knapsack made of same material as dress, stamp with Muffy figurine handle, features Muffy's signature with flower

Hoppy: rose-colored "signature" dress, two pockets screened with byline and telephone, rose colored organza headbow, darker pink Mary Janes

Telephone Handbag & Phonebook: black sueded telephone handbag, detachable receiver that ties to Hoppy's paw with ribbon, bag holds "very little black book"
**Headbow is attached on factory dressed bear.

Coloring and Activity Book

MerBear Porcelain

1999 Club Renewal Gift

Promotional Items

Muffy and Friends Stickers, Muffy and Friends Tatoos, Muffy and Hoppy Pencils, Salad Ballad and ABC Bookmarks, Muffy Purple and White Logo Balloons

ThumBearlina

Muffy's debut in mohair, costumed as the charming fairy tale character, ThumBearlina. She wears a cream silk taffeta gown, robe and cap embroidered with tiny ribbon roses, violets and French knot leaves. The gown is inset with antique lace and the cap ties with a hand-dyed silk ribbon. True to the classic story, she sleeps in a walnut shell cradle with a violet-petal silk embroidered mattress. Her bed is guarded by a green and gilt toad who holds up a chiffon and silk violet canopy. The piece is presented on an illustrated open fairy tale book.
One-of-a-kind for Disney Convention Auction

Sleep Over

Muffy: white cotton piqué nightie and matching sleep bonnet, both trimmed in lace; lavender flowers and butterflies embroidered on bonnet and gown, which also says "Good Night!"; lace trimmed pillow monogrammed with "M"

Hoppy: lace trimmed white cotton piqué night gown with matching sleep bonnet; yellow chamomile flowers embroidered on bonnet and edge of gown; "Sleep Tight" also embroidered on gown; cotton pillow monogrammed with "H"

Bunk Trunk: laminated playboard trunk with removable bunkbeds and custom print mattresses and pillows. A hanging rack and three drawers hold changes of clothes. 16-5/8" x 11-3/8" x 9-3/4"

Bunk Trunk Blanket Set: fleecy plaid blankets for Muffy and Hoppy

Muffy's Bear and Hoppy's Bunny in Pet-a-Porter Carrying Cases: fully jointed miniature stuffed animals in white lace-trimmed nighties in soft suitcases. Muffy's case in French Blue and Hoppy's in Wild Rose

Jam Session

Muffy: custom print polished cotton jumper, over a white blouse, features a plaid with bunches of strawberries, loop to hold wooden strainer, headbow** with two crocheted berries, red shoes with painted strawberries

Hoppy: pink strawberry print jumper, white cotton blouse with embroidered strawberry on collar, wooden scoop tied on front of her plaid apron, crocheted strawberries on her headbow, painted strawberries on front of red shoes

Jam Making Jar Set: three Muffy-sized plastic jars, strawberry design on lids, illustrated labels with three larger labels for your own jars; cotton piqué tea towel with strawberry-strewn embroidered "M"

Cookware Set: pot and pan set with lids; pot fits in pan to make double-boiler; cotton fabric oven mitt

Muffy's Stove: antique style tin stove with running water from faucet, utensil rack with three silver-toned kitchen accessories, decorated with Muffy and Hoppy hand-painted scenic tiles, two illustrated cardboard stools 10" x 9" x 5-3/8"

**Headbow is attached on factory dressed bear

All Spruced Up,
The Adirondack Collection

Cornelius: buffalo-check "wool" coat with wool toggle closures, two pockets accented with felt moose appliques; matching hat with sherpa lined ear flaps and red "wool" knit cuffed pants; brown and tan gum shoes

Alice: moose-print corduroy day dress under red "wool" hooded coat with black buttons, appliqued blue felt foxes on the pockets, green felt boots

Fuzzy: moose-print corduroy overalls under "wool" red jacket; two pockets appliqued with yellow felt finish; buffalo-check "wool" hat with sherpa lining, gum shoes

Fluffy: moose-print corduroy pinafore, red "wool" hooded coat, buffalo-check trim and wooden toggle buttons, two pockets with green felt tree appliques, green felt boots with knit trim

Muffy: buffalo-check "wool" coat with moose-print corduroy lined hood and pocket appliqued with green felt bear; winter pinafore is moose-print corduroy, red-laced boots are green felt

Hoppy: hooded buffalo-check "wool" coat with blue bunny felt applique; wears moose-print corduroy pinafore and green felt laced boots

Lulu: buffalo-check "wool" coat lined in moose-print corduroy; "wool" ear flap hat

Purrlie: buffalo-check "wool" buttoned coat with moose-print lining; yellow star hat edged in spruce green blanket stitching

Bruce the Spruce Moose: decorated with embroidered metallic ornaments and crowned with two blanket stitched yellow stars; red felt harness trimmed with bells, attaches to chair sled

Snowshoes, Scarf, and Mittens Set: scarf is red "wool" with tree and star applique, mittens are yellow fleece with blanket-stitched edges; wooden snowshoes with moose embroidery slip-on and tie over-boots

Sled: spruce green painted wood, screened with winter motifs, red reins attach to Spruce Moose's harness, 17" x 7" x 9"

Hangtag Note Folded gold and brown tag with birch branch border, includes name of the Collection and picture of Bruce

Hit the Road,
The Bearstream Trailer Collection

Muffy: postcard print cotton shirt and denim overalls, "Hit the Road" woven patch, printed cotton bandanna with map, hot green felt sunglasses sewn to bandanna, orange-flocked boots

Hoppy: postcard print shirt and bandanna match Muffy's, jeans decorated with "Hit the Road" woven patch, hot orange sunglasses sewn to her bandanna, orange-flocked boots

Lulu: sun visor, screened T-shirt featuring herself going over Niagara Falls in barrel

Purrlie: sun visor, screened T-shirt featuring "Purrlie Peaks"

Road Trip Gear: sleeping bag lined with quilted orange flannel, "Hit the Road" woven patch, camera and working flashlight, set of three postcards

Bearstream Trailer: laminated playboard, illustrated on both sides, holds picnic table, stove, two chairs, trailer is 24" x 11" 7"

Little Miss Muffy

Fifth Limited Edition Club Bear
- Kate Greenaway style "tuffet print" frock trimmed with lace, tied with velvet sash
- Ruffled polka-dot collar and bloomers
- Ribbon-tied bloomers
- Poke-style bonnet with velvet ribbon ties
- Spider wears polka-dot waistcoat with tails, plaid tie, and felt top hat
- Blue velvet tuffet trimmed with jacquard ribbon and yellow fringe
- Boxed • Factory dressed only
- First Annual Club Bear–previous Club Bears were limited by edition size. Little Miss Muffy was limited by time–the year 1999 is written on her label

The Millennium Collection:
From Dusk to Dawn

Collector's Edition Boxed Set Limited to 2000 Hand-numbered Pieces

Muffy: iridescent yellow taffeta gown with gold and orange silk organza overlay, rays of yellow glass seed beads, sun-shaped necklace, sun crown with beaded "2000," high heels, silk drawstring evening bag with beaded fringe

Hoppy: pale violet iridescent taffeta gown with matching silk organza overlay embroidered with glass beads, trimmed with wire-edged violet ribbon sash; violet glass beaded, crescent shaped crown, star necklace, silver glitter high heels; crescent moon shaped evening bag with iridescent button closure and beaded handle with millennium keepsake token

Factory Dressed Only

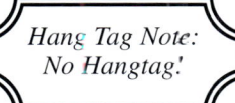

*Hang Tag Note:
No Hangtag!*

Muffy and Hoppy Millennium Porcelain Box

Handpainted with hinged lid; surprise message inscribed inside, 4-1/4" x 3" x 2-3/4"

Miss Muffy Belle's Hat Shop

Event Limited Edition
First Event Bear
Green taffeta plaid
Southern Belle-styled
dress with embroidered
yoke and attached taffeta
petticoat, matching plaid
headbow and black rib-
bon-tied sueded shoes.
Came with straw hat to
decorate at event
Factory Dressed Only

> *Hangtag Note*
> *Hat Box shaped tag in green,*
> *white, and purple with the*
> *Collection name and the*
> *words "Event Piece 1999,"*
> *tag is tied to Muffy's wrist*
> *with white ribbon*

Muffy Polar Bear, North Meets South

Holiday Limited Boxed Edition
Muffy: polar bear suit with
hood and stitched paws;
velboa penguin, working
plastic compass.
Factory Dressed Only

> *Hangtag Note*
> *Folded tag features Muffy's pen-*
> *guin friend, the Northern Lights*
> *and Collection name, inside is the*
> *Certificate of Authenticity*

Splash Party Collection

Muffy: daisy print flounced bathing suit made of cotton Lycra, white printed vinyl swim cap

Hoppy: one-piece striped tank racing suit made of cotton Lycra, white printed vinyl swim cap

Inflatable Rafts: pony and turtle, 11" x 7" x 4"

Fun-in-the-Sun Set: white printed terry cloth towel featuring Muffy and Hoppy, vinyl swim fins and tote bag with starfish, clamshell and wave print

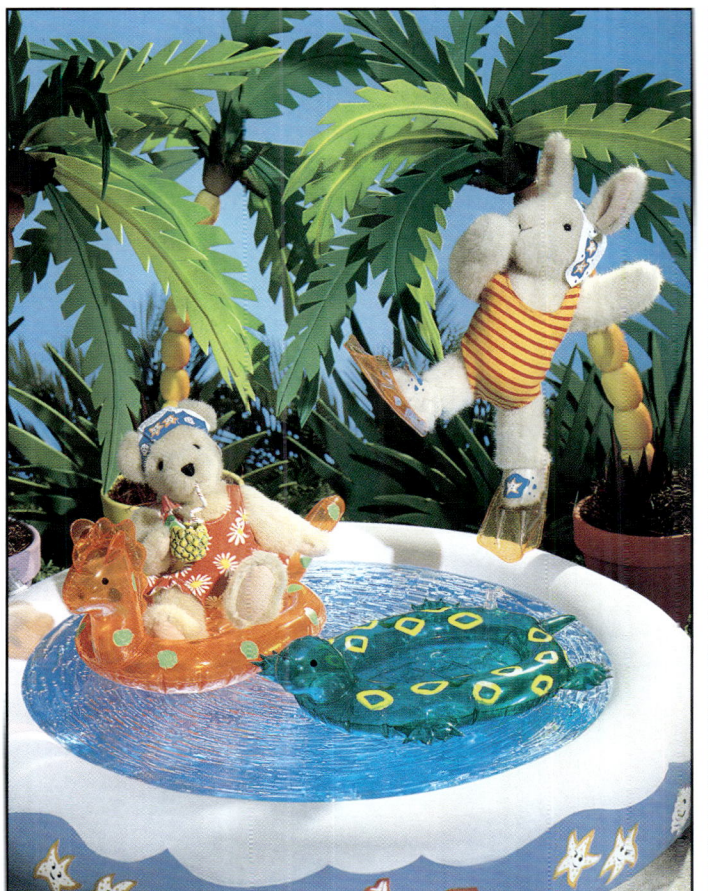

Hangtag Note
Folded tag in blue with sea side motif and Collection name

Squir'lfriend, A Walk in the Park

Muffy: cotton squirrel-and-acorn print smock dress with yellow collar, felt acorn hat, pair of yellow Mary Janes, yellow cotton squirrel-and-acorn print tote bag; Hazel Nutt the squirrel is brown velboa with furry plush tail and embroidered eyes

Hangtag Note
Folded tag in green and gold with large acorn in the center and Collection name

Hangtag Note Round folded tag in blue and white floral motif with Collection name

Garden Party

Cornelius & Fuzzy: brimmed straw hats, felt spectator shoes, flowered voile ties; Cornelius with crème twill pants, French blue vest over a blue and white striped shirt; Fuzzy with button-on knickers, French blue shirt with white collar and cuffs

Alice & Fluffy: rose bouquet print dresses with rose buttons and checked ribbon trim, bloomers that match the dresses, green felt shoes embroidered with roses, Garden Party natural straw hats with check bows

Muffy & Hoppy: Muffy in rosebud print dress with ribbon trim, collar, two trimmed pockets, wild rose bloomers, blue straw hat with ribbon trim**, embroidered blue felt shoes. Hoppy in wild rose print voile dress with ribbon trim, coordinating rosebud bloomers, blue embroidered felt shoes, and blue straw hat

Gazebo: illustrated playboard

Table Cloth and Chair Cushions: embroidered floral design, fits Bistrot table and chairs, comes with four napkins

Finger Sandwich Set: finger sandwich cutters, blue acrylic domed platter and four plates

**Hat is attached on factory dressed bear.

Gift To Go

2000

Full-cover gift boxes with ribbon handle, includes dressed Muffy "Deck the Halls with Bows and Dollies," Muffy Sleep Over Outfit, and Muffy's Bear in Pet-a-Porter Carrying Case

---

Muffy Club Logo Dress

2000

2000 Club Renewal Gift
- Will be added to new member kit for Fall 2000
- First club exclusive dress–gift with membership
- White twill pinafore with screen print of Muffy VanderBear Club logo on pocket, ribbon ties at back
- Smock-styled dress in Muffy's Signature print fabric
- Blue and white check organza headbow
- Flocked navy Mary Janes
- Available as outfit only

Muffy's Scrapbook

2000

- 48 pages of snippets, scraps, and stories of Muffy's life
- Illustrated, has interactive surprises
- 10" x 9" x ½"

A Bushel of Fun,
Apple Antics Collection

Muffy: Red Delicious cardigan knit sweater, hat topped with crocheted twig and leaf, "apple picking" print skirt, red Mary Janes

Hoppy: golden yellow, pull-over knit sweater and matching cap, red felt suspenders, "apple picking" print skirt, red Mary Janes

Apple Basket and Apples: Muffy-sized wooden bushel basket with metal handle, filled with resin apples

Apple Cart: painted wood with illustrated side panel

A Spot of Tea:
The Teacup Collection

Boxed 6th Muffy VanderBear Club Limited Edition

Muffy: cap-sleeve blue velvet dress with Spot of Tea embroidery, pillbox hat with organza ribbon, blue shoes with cameo design on toe, porcelain portrait cameo around neck, and Muffy sized teacup tied to paw

Factory Dressed Only

A Spot of Tea Teacup

Deep blue porcelain teacup and saucer matching Muffy's A Spot of Tea teacup, decorated with white bas-relief cameos of Muffy and Hoppy pouring tea

For Club Members Only

Artistes at Work

Muffy: blue linen artist's smock with screened multicolored paint smudges, double front pockets and red satin neck bow, black beret, paintbrush, framed mini paper portrait, black t-strap sandals

Hoppy: black cotton smock with screened photos of herself and Muffy, white t-strap sandals, black beret, daguerreotype print tied to wrist

Great Masterpieces Accessory Set: wooden easel, wooden paint palette, paper playboard reproductions; wooden box camera and tripod with retractable photo strip for Hoppy

Great Masterpieces Note Card Set: 20 cards, 4-1/2" x 6", includes "Hoppa Lisa," "Heavenly Buddies," "Muffy as Harlequin," and "Sunday Afternoon With The VanderBears"

Hangtag Note
Folded tag in blue with black border, includes name of Collection and dabs of paint

Cirque de la Lune:
A Looney Circus

Muffy: checkered taffeta jacket with screened sun, moon and star motif, pom-pom button, satin collar, balloon pantaloons, satin clown hat, felt lace-up clown shoes

Hoppy: jacket and balloon pants are mix of satins, taffetas, ruffles, and ribbons; one shoe with pom-pom, the other with lace ribbons, floppy hat with pom-pom

Lulu: curly plush lion suit with fringed mane and tail

Purrlie: multi-layered tutu of flowered organza, felt monogrammed crown

Oatsie: felt costume printed with moons and stars, plumed felt hat with grosgrain bridle

Circus Tent: canvas-covered playboard, four illustrated Cirque de la Lune posters, satin ribbons tie roof to the base, felt printed flag on top, 24" x 18-1/2" x 16-1/2"

Cirque de la Lune Accessory Set: decorated tin drum holds felt rings-a-fire and vinyl ball

Daisy Petals: She Loves Me

Hangtag Note
Four page folded blue tag with white and yellow daisy - inside is the game of "She Loves Me"

- Cotton daisy print dress with buttoned brushed tricot pocket flaps
- Yellow and white checked ribbon sash around waist, printed with "She Loves Me, She Loves Me Not"
- Brushed tricot and felt hat with checked ribbon to match waist sash
- Embroidered tricot slippers tied with ribbon

Deck the Halls
with Bows & Dollies

Muffy: green and red plaid taffeta dress with gold metallic thread running throughout, velvet bodice, satin headbow, flocked Mary Janes, satin bows on skirt. Handpainted porcelain "Muffy Dolly" ornament tied to wrist

Hoppy: plaid taffeta dress with cummerbund, velvet bodice, green flocked Mary Janes, satin headbow, with "Hoppy Dolly" porcelain ornament

Lulu: velvety coat decorated with red bows and plaid taffeta lining, satin headbow, porcelain "Lulu Dolly" ornament

Purrlie: wrapped inside red felt present tied with green satin bow and screen-printed with "Do Not Open Until Xmas", porcelain "Purrlie Dolly" ornament

Tree: 6 Muffy & friends hand-painted porcelain ornaments, porcelain "bear star" tree topper, gold-trimmed red bows, gold ball ornaments, pine cones, stands inside white-washed terra cotta base, 17" boxed

Fabeargé Egg Collection

Muffy: pink ombre ribbon taffeta dress with drop-waist and flounced skirt, pin-tucked front and lace-trimmed sash and hem; matching slippers trimmed with same pink satin as headbow; Fabeargé Egg in blue and gold enamel with rose trim, decorated with portrait of Muffy

Hoppy: blue ombre ribbon taffeta drop-waist dress with double-ruffled skirt, lace trim, front bow; blue satin slippers and headbow; pink and gold Fabeargé Egg with lily of the valley trim, features portrait of Hoppy

6 Imperial Eggs with Decorated Tin: feature sculpted resin portraits of Muffy and friends with decorative "enamel" trim; contained in illustrated tin box

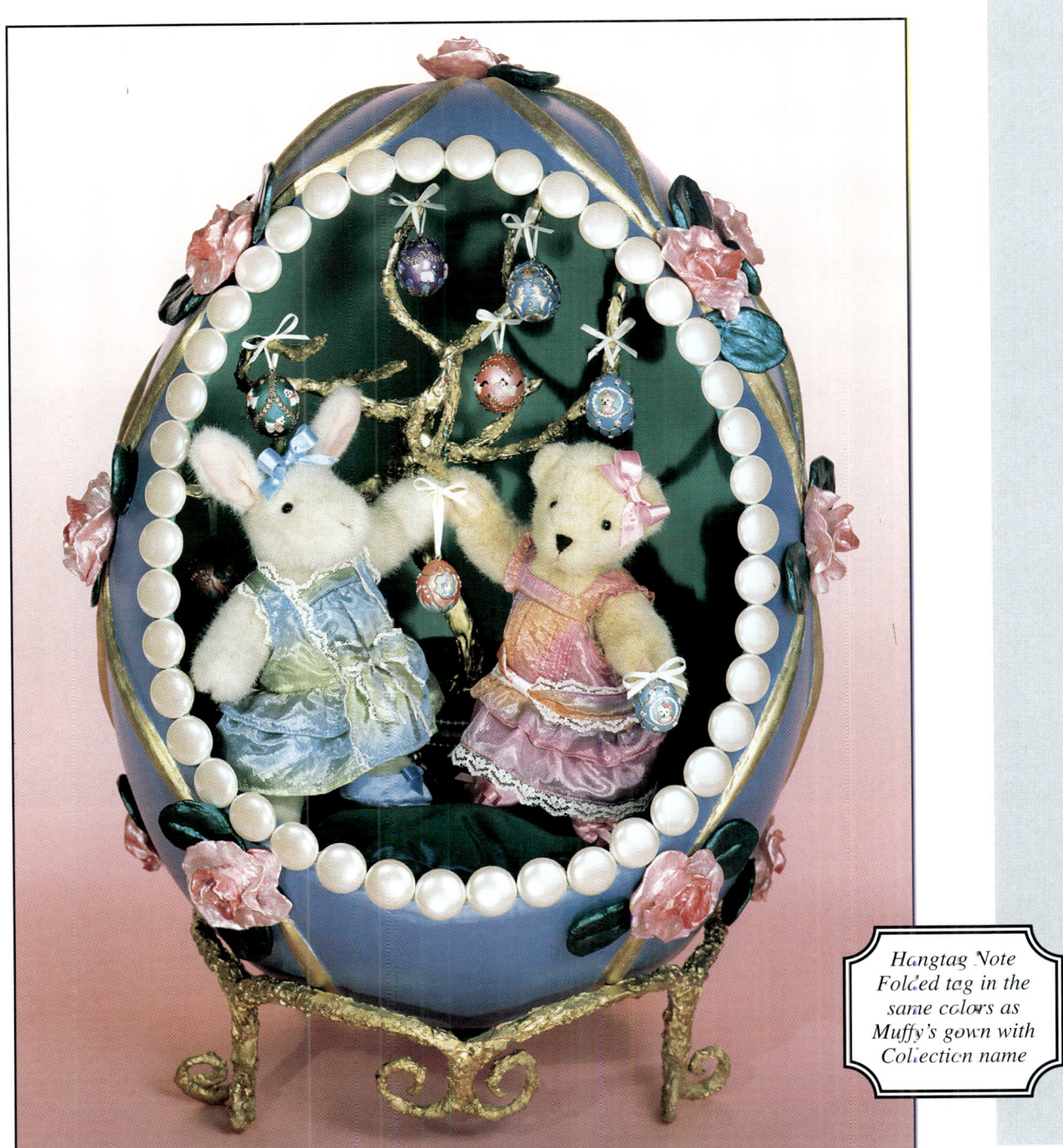

Hangtag Note
Folded tag in the same colors as Muffy's gown with Collection name

Muffy, Ahead of Her Time

Second Event Bear
- pink taffeta ball gown with crinoline under skirt and ribbon rose trim
- taffeta bolero jacket trimmed with organza ruffle
- taffeta clock face hat
- Event Limited Edition
- Factory Dressed Only

Event Accessory: "Muffy Ahead of Her Time" watch

Picnic in Provence

Muffy: Provençal print red sundress accented with sunflower buttons, double front pockets, ruffled hem and sleeves; wide brimmed burlap and Provençal print fabric sun hat; yellow espadrilles and market basket

Hoppy: Provençal print yellow sundress accented with sunflower buttons, burlap and Provençal fabric sunbonnet with checked ribbon; red espadrilles and burlap bag

Oatsie: yellow Provençal print fabric feedbag and double-sided saddlebasket

LuLu: Provençal print sunbonnet and sunflower trimmed bib

Purrlie: Provençal print sunhat and lavendar trimmed bib

Provençal Picnic Set: wicker basket with sunflower button enclosure; four tin plates, cotton tablecloth, four matching napkins, resin set of round bread, bowl of olives and berry tart

All Over in Clover: The Shamrock Collection

Muffy: shamrock-print green "cloveralls" with snap closures and pink and green woven patch on front bib; white hand-crocheted pullover sweater with a tie closure, features green edged trimming on the collar and sleeves; shamrock hat** made of felt, ladybug embroidered on front; pink Irish step-dancing shoes, laced with green ribbon

**Hat is attached on factory dressed bear.

Hangtag Note Folded tag in pink with Collection name, green shamrock, and lady bug

Muffy Winter Princess

Holiday Boxed Limited Edition

- Deep crimson velvet coat with glass beads and crystal-cut buttons
- Coat, hat, muff and white felt lace-up boots trimmed with snowy white plush
- Beaded snowflake and silver trimmed organza bow on front of her hat
- Comes inside glittered box with illustrated winter forest scene with a certificate of authenticity
- A Muffy Holiday Limited Edition piece
- Factory Dressed Only

Hangtag Note Rectangular folded hangtag, watercolor blue background with gold house at top and tree branch border

The Muffy VanderBear® Club

Muffy's Fan Club started in 1990 and now has over 22,000 members! Upon joining, members receive a Club Kit and a free gift each year when they renew. Through the years, a soft cover Photo Album, with all Muffy Collections pictured, was included in the Club Kit. This Photo Album was updated three times. In the first album, some of the dates were wrong, but these were later corrected. In 1996 the soft cover album was replaced with the 2 ring, hard cover binder. In 1998 a separate Muffy Kid's Club was started.

Soft Cover Photo Albums
#1-1990: Includes Collections through Spring 1991, cover with Muffy Gibearny & outfits
#2-1993: Includes Collections through Fall 1993, cover with Muffy and friends
#3-1995: Includes Collections through Fall 1995, cover with new Muffy ribbon logo

In 1996, the soft cover album was replaced with a hard cover 2-ring canvas binder, called a Collection Album, featuring picture inserts. It is the gift for all new and renewing members starting in 1996 and is to be updated yearly with renewal. The 1996 New Membership Kit also includes a new set of Muffy Stationary that current members can purchase. Members have an opportunity to purchase extra gifts after the first year they are offered. The following chart lists all of the gifts that were included with memberships and renewals. We have included the price for those items presently available and the page number for a description.

Date	Membership Gifts	Cost	Page
1990	Club Kit I, below left (original price $12)	Retired	36
1992	Scarf/Bandana, below right	$8	51
1993	Tote Bag, below right (original price $9.50)	Retired	59
1994	Rose Frame, below right	$11	68
1995	Fan Box, below right (original price $10)	Retired	74
1995	Photo Album #3, soft cover	Retired	126
1996	Club Kit II	$25	86
1996	Collection Album with Binder	$15	86
1996	New Club Stationery & Stickers	$7.50	86
1997	Muffy Pouch	$10	94
1998	Travel Trunk Clock	$10	101
1999	Brooch replaced Pendant in Kit	$6	-
1999	MerBear Porcelain Box	$12	109
2000	Logo Dress	-	117

Club Merchandise

In addition to the gifts that come with membership, Club members also have an opportunity to purchase other Club merchandise. The most popular of these are the exclusive limited edition Muffys. Members receive a redemption certificate for the Club Muffy and are requested to place their order through a North American Bear dealer. So far there have been three of these special Muffys offered to members. A special surprise for 1996 was the first T-Shirt offered to Charter Members only.

Other benefits of the Muffy Club:

- Three issues of Fanfare featuring stories and information about Muffy
- Three issues of the North American Bear Newsletter
- Pen Pals program
- Free North American Bear catalogs to keep you up-to-date on new collections
- Wanted & Fur Sale service for members to buy, sell, & trade retired Nabco products

Date	Club Limited Edition Muffys	Page
1991	Muffy Butterfly, numbered LE 10000	46
1993	Muffy Rose, numbered LE 10000	63
1995	Princess and The Pea, numbered LE 15000	75
1997	Muffy MerBear, numbered LE 15000	98
1999	Little Miss Muffy, LE	112
2000	A Spot of Tea: The Teacup Collection, LE	118
Other Club Merchandise		
1996	T-Shirt for Charter Members, only 4100 offered	88
1996	T-Shirt for all Club Members	88
1998	Sweatshirt	-
Birthday Cards		
Club Members also receive Birthday Cards from Muffy, shown at left.		
1993	Accordion Fold-Out	59
1994	Muffy Flying	68
1995	Happy Birthday Figures	74
1996	Birthday Cake	88
1997	Happy Birthday Muffy Pop-out	94
1998	Life is One Big Dress-Up	-
1999	Happy Birthday Fold-over	-
2000	Muffy & Hoppy Millennium with token	-

MUFFY VANDERBEAR CLUB
401 N. Wabash, Suite 500
Chicago, IL 60611
1-800-682-3427

Promotional Products – not part of club membership

1996 Collection Binder, Stationary, and Stickers

Muffy VanderBear®: The Bare Facts

The following information is meant only as a guide for collectors. Based on our research, we have included dates when we think specific Muffys might have been made and a few examples of Muffys that came factory dressed on a bear with that tag. The tag samples show the front and the back of the tag and are printed exactly as they appear on the bears. Many collectors have contributed to the accuracy of this information, but there will be some variations and examples that may have been missed. We are aware that there were a few Muffys manufactured with a rare side tag, but have not included it in this guide. When we saw this tag several years ago, on a Christening Muffy, we were novice collectors and neglected to note the type of tag for future reference.

#1 Tush Tag: 1984-1986, Korea

Muffy was born with a large looped tag on her tush, which later became known as the "Tush Tag" Muffy. Muffy herself was slightly under 7 inches tall with very short fur, tiny face features, small hips with legs fitted tightly together, and tan in color. The "Tush Tag" Muffy is the most sought after by collectors.

Tush Tag Muffy, front and back.

VANDERBEAR FAMILY®™ ©1982 ALL RIGHTS RESERVED NORTH AMERICAN BEAR CO., INC. N.Y. CHICAGO 312/943-1061	ALL NEW POLYESTER FILLING SURFACE WASHABLE MASS., OHIO, MAINE PA. (NY) 648 MADE IN KOREA DESIGNED BY: BARBARA ISENBERG

Actual Size (1-3/8" x 7/8")

Tush tag bears can be found factory dressed in:
Christening I • Christening II • Cruisewear • Red Flannel

#2 Tiny Loop Tag: 1985-1987, Tag high on back, Korea

This Muffy was like the "Tush Tag" Muffy in height, but her fur was slightly longer and her hips were wider. Starting with this Muffy, the tags were placed high on the back.

*On some variations, the first line also has the trademark symbol: MUFFY VANDER BEARS®™

Tush Tag on left, Tiny Loop on right.

MUFFY VANDERBEARS® ©1982 ALL RIGHTS RESERVED NORTH AMERICAN BEAR. CO., INC. CHICAGO ILL 312-329-0020	ALL NEW MATERIALS STUFFED WITH 100% POLYESTER MA, OHIO MEPA (NY) 648 MADE IN KOREA DESIGNED BY BARBARA ISENBERG

Approx. Size is 3/4" x 3/8"

Examples of some bears factory dressed with this tag:
**Christening I & II • Cruisewear • Day In The Country I • Nutcracker
Red Flannel • Taffeta • Valentine I • Witch**

#3 Small Loop Tag: 1986-1989, Korea

During this period, Muffy began to grow. She was between 7-1/4 and 7-1/2 inches tall and similar to the Tiny Loop Tag Muffy, except that her fur was a little longer and plusher, resulting in a softer, shinier look.

Front and back views of #2 tiny Loop (on left), #3 Small Loop (center), and #4 Small Cut Loop (on right).

VANDER BEAR FAMILY®
©1982 NORTH AMERICAN
BEAR CO., INC.
CHICAGO IL 312/329-0020
ALL RIGHTS RESERVED
BARBARA ISENBERG DESIGNS
COSTUMES BY ODL BAUER

ALL NEW MATERIALS
STUFFED WITH 100% POLYESTER
MA, OHIO ME PA (NY) 648
MADE IN KOREA

Examples of some bears
factory dressed with this tag:
Black Cat with heavy glitter
Bunny with wicker basket • Cruisewear
Day In The Country • Furrier & Ives
Nutcracker • Out of it in Africa • Taffeta
Tree Trimming • Valentine I & II
Witch • Red Flannel

Approx. Size 1" x 1/2"

#4 Small Cut Loop Tag: 1988-1990, Korea

Like the Small Loop Tag II, except that it was cut in two. By this time Muffy had grown to 7-1/2 inches tall, with even wider hips and legs that were set far apart. Her fur was the same as the Loop Tag Bear.

VANDERBEAR FAMILY®
©1982 NORTH AMERICAN
BEAR CO., INC.
CHICAGO IL 312/329-0020
ALL RIGHTS RESERVED
BARBARA ISENBERG DESIGNS
COSTUMES BY ODL BAUER

ALL NEW MATERIALS
STUFFED WITH 100% POLYESTER
MA, OHIO ME PA (NY) 648
MADE IN KOREA

Examples of some bears factory dressed with this tag:
Angel • Black Cat • Tree Trimming
Christening III • Furrier & Ives • St. Patrick's
Valentine II • Valentine III, white

Size varied between 3/4" x 1/2" and 7/8" x 1-1/2"

#5 Small Cut Loop Tag II: 1989-1990, Korea

Like the previous Small Loop Tag II with a cute, small face and small ears.

MUFFY VANDERBEAR®
©1982 NORTH AMERICAN
BEAR CO., INC.
CHICAGO, IL 312/329-0020
ALL RIGHTS RESERVED
BARBARA ISENBERG DESIGNS
COSTUMES BY ODL BAUER

ALL NEW MATERIALS
100% POLYESTER STUFFING
SURFACE WASHABLE
REG. NO. PA. — 2865 (KR)
MADE IN KOREA

Examples of some bears factory dressed with this tag:
St. Patrick's
Bunny

Approx. Size is 1" x 1/2"

#6 Long Single Tag: 1989-1992, Korea

At this time Muffy's fur took on a greenish cast when compared to the previous tan. She was still 7-1/2 inches tall, but with a larger chin and narrow face. Some collectors unflatteringly refer to this as a "doggy face." But don't tell Muffy!

Examples of some bears factory dressed with this tag:
Alpine • Back to School • Ballet Recital
Bal Masque • Beach • Black Cat, glitter
Chick, No black outline on eyes
Cruisewear, snap & Velcro
Day in the Country I & II
Down on the Farm • Dutch Treat
Fir Tree • Furrier & Ives
Gibearny • Gypsy • High Tea
Musical Soiree • Out of it in Africa
Pilgrim • Snow Bear • Sweet Dreams
Tree Trimming • Valentine II
Valentine III, cream • Wild West

#3 Small loop Muffy on left. #6 Long Single Tag Muffy from Korea on right.

ALL NEW MATERIALS
100% POLYESTER STUFFING
SURFACE WASHABLE
REG. NO. PA. — 2865 (KR)
MADE IN KOREA
PLEASE REMOVE RIBBON, TAG
AND ALL TRIMMINGS BEFORE
GIVING TO SMALL CHILD

MUFFY VANDERBEAR®
©1982 NORTH AMERICAN
BEAR CO., INC.
CHICAGO, IL 312-329-0020
ALL RIGHTS RESERVED
BARBARA ISENBERG DESIGNS
COSTUMES BY ODL BAUER

Approx. Size is 1-1/4" x 1/2"

#7 Long Single Tag II: 1991-1992, Indonesia

Muffy's fur and size were like the previous bear with the Long Single Tag, but she was made in Indonesia. These were made with both small and large chins.

Examples of some bears factory dressed
with this tag:
Ballet Recital (some with "Cowlike" face)
Bal Masqué • Black Cat (glitter)
Beach • Christening IV • Gypsy
High Tea • Musical Soireé • Paw de Deux
Out Of It In Africa, Velcro
Yankee Doodle

#6 Long Single Tag Muffy from Korea on left.
#7 Long Single Tag II Muffy from Indonesia on right.

MUFFY VANDERBEAR®
©1982 NORTH AMERICAN
BEAR CO., INC.
CHICAGO, IL 312/329-0020
ALL RIGHTS RESERVED
BARBARA ISENBERG DESIGNS
COSTUMES BY ODL BAUER

ALL NEW MATERIALS
100% POLYESTER STUFFING
SURFACE WASHABLE
REG. NO. PA. - 2865 (KR)
MADE IN INDONESIA
PLEASE REMOVE RIBBON, TAG
AND ALL TRIMMINGS BEFORE
GIVING TO SMALL CHILD

Approx. Size is 1-1/2" x 5/8"

#8 Double Tag I: 1991-1993, Indonesia

This tag was the same as the single tag with an additional **second, wider tag** that included information on fiber content and a removal warning (in English on one side and French on the other). Muffy's fur and size were the same.

MUFFY VANDERBEAR® ©1982 NORTH AMERICAN BEAR CO., INC. CHICAGO, IL 312/329-0020 ALL RIGHTS RESERVED BARBARA ISENBERG DESIGNS COSTUMES BY ODL BAUER	ALL NEW MATERIALS 100% POLYESTER STUFFING SURFACE WASHABLE REG. NO. PA. - 2865 (KR) MADE IN INDONESIA PLEASE REMOVE RIBBON, TAG AND ALL TRIMMINGS BEFORE GIVING TO SMALL CHILD

Approx. Size is 1-1/2" x 5/8"

Examples of some factory dressed with this tag:
**Bal Masque • Beach • Down on the Farm
Easter Fantasy • Gibearny • High Tea, Velcro
Mommy & Me • Musical Soireé
Out of it in Africa, Velcro • Paw De Deux
Sweet Dreams • Yankee Doodle**

#9 Double Tag II: 1991-1994, Indonesia

The narrow tag below was used again with the second wider tag described in #8. This tag is on **both the greenish/tan bear and the "new fur" Muffy** that came out in 1993 (more tan in color, similar to the older Muffy).
*There are also examples of this same tag from Korea. *On some examples the word "Polyester" is followed by "fiber".

MUFFY VANDERBEAR® ©1982 NORTH AMERICAN BEAR CO., INC. CHICAGO, IL 312/329-0020 ALL RIGHTS RESERVED BARBARA ISENBERG DESIGNS COSTUMES BY ODL BAUER	ALL NEW MATERIALS STUFFING: 100% POLYESTER SURFACE WASHABLE REG. NO. PA. - 2865 (KR) MADE IN INDONESIA NOT RECOMMENDED FOR CHILDREN UNDER THREE YEARS DUE TO SMALL PARTS & TRIM

Approx. Size is 1-1/2" x 1/2"

Examples of some bears factory dressed with this tag:
**Alpine • Back to School • Ballet Recital • Bal Masque • Beach
BeeKeeping • Black Cat • Bunny • Chick • Christening IV
Day in the Country • Down on the Farm • Dutch Treat
Easter Fantasy • Equestrienne • Flower Festival • Gibearny
GingerBear • Grand Tour • Gypsy • Highland Fling • High Tea
Kyoto • Mommy & Me • Musical Soireé • Out of it in Africa
Picnic • Pilgrim • Queen of Hearts • Rainy Day • St. Patrick's
Sewing Lesson • Snowflake • Sweet Dreams • Valentine II
Valentine III (cream) • Wild West • Yankee Doodle**

#10 Double Tag III: 1991-1993, Korea

Special tag for **Muffy Butterfly** has the edition number written in by hand. The back is blank.

MUFFY VANDERBEAR® ©1982 NORTH AMERICAN BEAR CO., INC. CHICAGO, IL 312/329-0020 ALL RIGHTS RESERVED BARBARA ISENBERG DESIGNS COSTUMES BY ODL BAUER	ALL NEW MATERIALS 100% POLYESTER STUFFING SURFACE WASHABLE REG. NO. PA 2865 (KR) MADE IN KOREA PLEASE REMOVE RIBBON, TAG AND ALL TRIMMINGS BEFORE GIVING TO A SMALL CHILD	MUFFY BUTTERFLY LTD. ED._____ OF 10,000 MUFFY VANDERBEAR® CLUB ©1991 NORTH AMERICAN BEAR CO., INC.

Approx. Size is 1-3/4" x 1/2"   Approx. Size is 1-1/4" x 3/4"

#11 Double Tag IV: 1992-1995, China

This time the two tags were **exactly the same size**. The first tag was like the sample below. The second tag contained the same fiber information and warnings as previously described, except the words are printed in a different layout. These were all the "new fur" Muffys. Some feel that the faces on these were not as cute as the "new fur" Indonesian Muffys.

MUFFY VANDERBEAR® ©1982 NORTH AMERICAN BEAR CO., INC. Chicago, IL 312/329-0020 All Rights Reserved Barbara Isenberg Designs Costumes by Odl Bauer TF 26-0392	All new materials Stuffing: 100% polyester fiber Surface washable Reg. No. PA 648 Made in China Not recommended for children under three years due to small parts & trim

Approx. Size is 1" x 3/4"

Examples of some bears factory dressed with this tag:
**Back to School • Ballet Recital • Bal Masque
Beach • Black Cat • Bunny
Cherry Pie • Dutch Treat • Equestrienne
Farm • Grand Tour • Highland Fling
Paw De Deux • Pilgrim**

#12 Single Tag: 1993, No Country Name

This special tag for **Muffy Rose** has the edition number written in by hand and is blank on the back.

> MUFFY ROSE
> Ltd. Ed.____ of 10,000
> Muffy VanderBear® Club
> ©1993 North American Bear Co., Inc.

Approx. Size is 1-1/2" x 3/4"

#13 Double Tag V: 1994-1996, Indonesia

These again are "new fur" Muffys. The second tag is shorter, but wider, with the same fiber content and warning information described originally.

Left to right:
#9 Double Tag II Muffy from Indonesia with old fur, on left.
#13 Double Tag V Muffy from Indonesia with new fur, center.
#11 Double Tag IV Muffy from China with new fur, on right.

> MUFFY VANDERBEAR®
> © 1982 NORTH AMERICAN BEAR CO., INC.
> Chicago, IL 312/329-0020 - All Rights Reserved
> Made in Indonesia • Barbara Isenberg Designs
> Costumes by odl Bauer & Katya Bauer
> This product meets or exceeds all government safety regulations. Not recommended for children under 3 years of age. If a child under 3 has access to this product, remove all tags, buttons, trim and accessories

> All new materials
> Stuffing: 100% polyester fiber
> remove all trim before washing, Surface wash with cold water. Air-dry, brush gently if necessary
> Reg. No. PA 2865 (KR)

Approx. Size is 1-3/4" x 3/4"

Examples of some bears factory dressed with this tag:

All Paws   Anniversary • Bathtime • Beach • Boudoir • Bunny • Candy C'Angel • Checkmates • Chick • Clubhouse • Countess Muffula Easter Fantasy • Flower Festival • Happy Birthday • Highland Fling • Mozart • Muffy of the North • North Pole/Santa • Pajama Game Paw de Deux • Pilgrim • Queen of Hearts • Rainy Day • Reading • ReinBear • St. Patrick's • Spring Bonnets • Take a Hike Valentine III, white • Egg Painting • Yankee Doodle • Sewing Lesson

Both tags are exactly the same size with one as described below and the second with fiber information and warnings.

Left to right:
Original 6-3/4" Tush Tag Muffy on left and #14 new 7-1/2" Muffy on right

*Later versions of the tag below had the word water on the next line and the bottom number varied:
TF59-0594
TF58-0594
TF51-0594
TF24-0294

Examples of some bears factory dressed with this tag:
**Beach • Bunny • Cherry Pie • Christening IV
Czarina Muffina • Easter Fantasy
Fortune Teller • Kyoto • Pajama Game
Paw de Deux • Picnic • St. Patrick's
Sleddin' & Skidaddlin'**

Left to right:
The three different Muffy furs:
Original #3 on left, greenish fur #9
in center, new tan #14 on right.

All new materials
Stuffing: 100% polyester fiber
remove all trim before washing.
Surface wash with cold water
Air-dry, brush gently if necessary.
Reg. No. PA 4345 (HK)

MUFFY VANDERBEAR®
© 1982 NORTH AMERICAN BEAR CO., INC.
Chicago, IL 312/329-0020 - All Rights Reserved
Made in China • Barbara Isenberg Designs
Costumes by Odl Bauer & Katya Bauer
This product meets or exceeds all government
safety regulations. Not recommended for
children under 3 years of age. If a child under
3 has access to this product, remove all tags,
buttons, trim and accessories
TF25-0294

Approx. Size is 1" x 3/4"

#15 Triple Tag: 1995-1996, Indonesia

Princess Muffy and the Pea has 3 tags: (1) exactly like Indonesian tag #13 described earlier, (2) a shorter, wider tag with fiber information and warnings, (3) a special tag as described at right, with the edition number written in by hand.

Princess Muffy
and The Pea
LTD. ED.____ of 15,000
Muffy VanderBear® Club
©1995 North American Bear Co., Inc.

Approx. size is 1-1/2" x 3/4"

MUFFY VANDERBEAR®
© 1994 NORTH AMERICAN BEAR CO., INC.
Chicago, IL 312/329-0020
All Rights Reserved
Made in China
Barbara Isenberg Designs
Costumes by Odl Bauer

TF145-1193

All new materials
Stuffing: 100% polyester fiber
Machine wash, cool (in pillowcase)
mild detergent.
Tumble dry, low (in pillowcase).

This product is recommended for all ages and meets or exceeds all government safety regulations.

#16 Double Tag VII: 1995, China

Both tags are exactly the same size with one as described at left and the second with fiber information and warnings. *This was the first time that Muffy's tag has stated that she could be placed in the washing machine and dryer and that she was recommended for all ages.*

Approx. Size is 1" x 3/4"

Examples of some bears factory dressed with this tag: **New England Country Christmas**

#17 Double Tag VIII: 1995-1998, China

Both tags are exactly the same size with one as described at right and the second with fiber information and warnings.

Examples of some bears
factory dressed with this tag:
**Hearts & Flowers • Muffy Mouse
Portrait in Black & White • Spring Bonnets
Sweets for the Sweet**

MUFFY VANDERBEAR®
© 1994 NORTH AMERICAN BEAR CO., INC.
Chicago, IL 312/329-0020
All Rights Reserved
Made in China
Barbara Isenberg Designs
Costumes by Odl Bauer

TF145-1193

All new materials
Stuffing: 100% polyester fiber
Remove all trim before washing.
Surface wash with cold water. Air-dry, brush gently if necessary.
Reg. No. PA-4345 (HK)
Please remove ribbon, tags, and all trimming before giving to a small child.

Approx. Size is 1" x 3/4"

MUFFY VANDERBEAR®
© 1982 NORTH AMERICAN BEAR CO., INC.
Chicago, IL 312/329-0020 — All Rights Reserved
Made in China
Costumes by Odl Bauer & Katya Bauer
This product meets or exceeds all government safety regulations. Not recommended for children under 3 years of age. If a child under 3 has access to this product, remove all tags, buttons, trim and accessories
TF118-1095

Approx. Size is 1-3/4" x 3/4"

#18 Triple Tag: 1996, China

Muffy Pierrot has 3 tags: (1) as described below with her edition number written in by hand — Pierrot was not a Club bear, so the word Club is a mistake, (2) the regular tag with front and back described at left and below, (3) the usual tag with fiber information and warnings, not shown.

All new materials
Stuffing: 100% polyester fiber
Remove all trim before washing.
Surface wash with cold water.
Air-dry, brush gently if necessary.
Reg. No. PA-4345 (HK)

Approx.
Size is 1-3/4" x 3/4"

Muffy Pierrot
Ltd. Ed.___ of 20,000
Muffy VanderBear® Club
©1996 North American Bear Co., Inc.

Approx. Size is 1-1/2" x 3/4"

#19 Triple Tag: 1996-1997, China

The first tag is as described at right. The remaining 2 tags are slightly larger and contain the fiber information. These 2 fiber information tags appear to have been one tag in the form of a loop that have been cut apart…the backs are blank.

Examples of some bears
factory dressed with this tag:
**Cheerleading • Foolish Ghoulish
Happy Birthday • Lemonade • Mercy Me
New England • Paris Bistrot • Paw de Deux
Portrait in Black & White • Salad Ballad
Square Dancing • Rainy Day**

MUFFY VANDERBEAR®
© 1982 NORTH AMERICAN BEAR CO., INC.
Chicago, IL 312/329-0020 • All Rights Reserved
Made in China • Barbara Isenberg Designs
Costumes by Odl Bauer & Katya Bauer
This product meets or exceeds all government safety regulations. Not recommended for children under 3 years of age. If a child under 3 has access to this product, remove all tags, buttons, trim and accessories
TF120-1095

All new materials
Stuffing: 100% polyester fiber
Remove all trim before washing.
Surface wash with cold water.
Air-dry, brush gently if necessary.
Reg. No. PA-4345 (HK)

Approx. Size is 1" x 3/4". *TF number varies.

Muffy In The Spotlight

GOLDEN TEDDY
NOMINATIONS AND AWARDS

Year	Nominated	Won?
1990	Fir Tree	Yea!
1990	Alice Musical Soiree	Yea!
1991	Gypsy (Fortune Teller)	Yea!
1992	Dutch Treat	Yea!
1993	Kyoto Blossoms	Boo!
1994	Boudoir	Boo!
1995	All Paws On Deck	Boo!
1996	Happy Birthday	Boo!
1999	Muffy Cinbearella *one-of-a-kind*	Boo!

TOBY NOMINATIONS

1990	Back to School
1991	Wild West
1994	Queen of Hearts
1995	All Paws On Deck
1999	PocaHoppy

MUFFY ON PAW-RADE

Muffy loves appearing in the Macy's Thanksgiving Day Parade!

1991	Bal Masque	1996	Pilgrim
1992	Alpine	1997	Pilgrim
1993	Grand Tour	1998	Pilgrim & PocaHoppy
1994	Pilgrim		
1995	New England Country Christmas with Purrlie	1999	Pilgrim & PocaHoppy

MORE AWARDS

1992:	Muffy Cherry Pie - Family Fun Toy of the Year
1995:	Muffy - nominated for a Collector's Choice Award in the category of Best Manufactured Teddy Bear.
	Muffy - First Runner Up in the Plush category of *Specialty Retailer Magazine's* Top Toys of 1995.
1997:	Muffy Cherry Pie - Dr. Toy's Best Classic Toy
	Mercy Me - Middle Georgia Parenting's Best Holiday Toys
	Muffy - Playthings Magazine's Top Ten List of Best Selling Toys in Specialty Stores
1998:	Muffy & Hoppy - Oppenheim Toy Portfolio Gold Seal
1999:	Blue Pagoda - Oppenheim Toy Portfolio's Platinum Seal
1999:	Hit The Road - Georgia Family Best Toys
2000:	Bunk Trunk - Oppenheim Toy Portfolio Gold Seal

More Muffy Trivia

SPECIAL BEARS

There have been a few special VanderBears that were made for a specific store or occasion. The most well-known of these is *Garlee*. *Garlee* was created in 1989 as an exclusive for *Diana's Bear Den* and the **Gilroy Garlic Festival** in California. This special white bear was made from the same pattern as Muffy and wears a lilac princess costume with a banner that reads, **Gilroy Garlic Festival, 1989**. Limited to 2500, *Garlee* originally sold for $40. Although she is not considered a Muffy, some collectors refer to *Garlee* as Muffy's cousin and she is quite collectible.

In 1991, there was a limited edition boxed set available only from **FAO Schwarz**. This was the same Muffy and Hoppy that appeared in all of the stores, but they were packaged in a special box. The set included dressed Muffy & Hoppy *Ballet Recital* with *Paw de Deux* outfits and was priced between $125 and $150. **Neiman Marcus** also had an exclusive Muffy set. In 1995 they featured Muffy *Grand Tour*, Lulu with her Tag and Leash, 4 Muffy outfits, and 4 Cameo Hangers all packaged in the Travel Trunk for a price of $198. In 1999, **FAO Schwarz** offered the *Adirondack Set* of Muffy, Lulu, Bruce and the Sled for $135.

Fluffy and Fuzzy have also made special appearances in the past years. Fluffy *Day in the Country* was made for the **San Francisco Music Box Co.** with a music box in her tummy that plays the *Teddy Bears' Picnic*, in 1999 her value was around $250. Fuzzy also got a real "kick" out of being dressed for the *World's Cup*.

WHAT ARE MUFFY'S CHARMS?

Special Accessories that came in her pocket and were described as "Muffy's Charms" in the catalogs.

Tree Trimming Gingerbread Cookie	1989
Gibearny Paint Tube	1990

More Muffy Trivia

The Vanderbears Love to Travel!

1988	Africa
1990	France
1991	The Wild West
1992	The Alps
1993	Scotland
1993	Kyoto, Japan
1994	The North Pole
1995	The Tropics
1997	Paris
2000	Provence
2000	Pennsylvania Dutch Country

Vanderbear Firsts

1st Collection without Muffy - Classic Velvet, 1983
1st Muffy - Christening, 1984
1st Alice & Cornelius Alone - Rembearances, 1990
1st Hoppy - Back to School, 1990
1st Oatsie - Wild West, 1991
1st Lulu - Highland Fling, 1993
1st Purrlie - New England, 1995, kitten attached to Muffy
1st Hoppy Alone - Cocoa Bunny, 1996
1st Bruce - Adirondack, 1999
1st Mohair Muffy – Thumbearlina, one-of-a-kind for Disney Auction

Who Came Factory Dressed Only?

Muffy Christening I	1983
Scottie VanderDog	1989
Oatsie Wild West	1991
Muffy's Farm Friends	1992
Bud & Rose	1993
Lulu Highland Fling	1993
Cornelius & Alice Paint the Town Red	1996
Purrlie Lemonade	1997
Cornelius & Alice Puttering Around	1997
Bruce The Spruce Moose	1999
All Event Editions	
All Boxed Christmas and Limited Editions	
All Club Editions	

What Came As An Outfit Only?

Muffy and Hoppy Underthings	1991
Muffy and Hoppy Sleddin' Back Packs and Accessories	1995
Portrait In Black and White Gifts	1997
Club Renewal Dress	2000

Where Can You Find the Vanderbears?

VanderBear Manor: Where the family lives most of the year
Pawtucket: New England location of their summer home, their favorite pastime is sailing
Bearatoga: Pony country near Pawtucket
Bearkshires: Location of "Aunt" Beartrice's farm
MacVanderBearn Castle: Originally known as Castle Wee Bairn in Scotland
Bearmont: Location of their rustic farmhouse
VandeBear Valley: Where Little BearPeep watches her sheep
VanderBear Lodge: Adirondack retreat

Oops! Even Muffy Makes Mistakes!

(But not very often.)

• Some of the dates in Muffy's first **Club Photo Album** were wrong, these were later corrected.
• The 1989 Catalog showed **Muffy Angel's** halo without stars...but all of the **Muffy Angels** came with stars on their halos.
• **Scottie VanderDog** is pictured in the 1989 catalog with a solid green bow, but it was plaid when he arrived. In the Spring 1990 catalog, the Scottie Dog is pictured with a leash, but it was never produced....perhaps because he ran away!
• The 1991 Catalog pictures Muffy **Wild West** with felt boots, but she appeared with red Mary Janes..
• In 1992 the **Picnic Collection** is pictured in the catalog with a wicker **Picnic Basket** for Muffy. Unfortunately only a paper one was available.
• In the Fall of 1992, the catalog listed the **Pop-up Cards** with the inclusion of *Bal Masque*, but this was not part of the set.
• Muffy's and Hoppy's **Take a Hike** hangtags were around their necks, not on their wrists as stated in the 1996 catalog.
• The tag on the bare Muffy that comes factory dressed as **Pierrot** reads, "Muffy VanderBear® Club." Pierrot was not a Club bear; it was a limited edition for all collectors.
• The **Paper Maché Ornaments** pictured in the 1998 Winter Catalog were never produced.
• Muffy's Cheerleading Outfit has red buttons not white as shown in the Fall 1996 Catalog.

Special Editions At A Glance

CHRISTMAS COLLECTIONS

1985	Red Flannel
1986	Taffeta
1987	Nutcracker Suite
1988	Furrier and Ives
1989	Tree Trimming
1990	Musical Soiree
1991	Bal Masque
1992	Alpine
1993	Highland Fling
1994	North Pole
1995	New England Country Christmas
1996	Christmas Carol
1997	Portrait In Black & White
1998	Grand VanderBall
1999	Adirondack, All Spruced Up
2000	Deck the Halls With Bows & Dollies

BOXED CHRISTMAS MUFFYS

1989	Angel
1990	Fir Tree
1991	SnowBear
1992	GingerBear
1993	Snowflake
1994	Muffy of the North
1995	Mouse
1996	ReinBear
1997	Candy C'angel
1998	Plum Fairy
1999	Polar Bear
2000	Winter Princess

BOXED SPECIAL EDITIONS

1991	Butterfly, Club, 10,000
1992	Rose, Club, 10,000
1994	Anniversary, Muffy's 10th
1995	Princess and The Pea, Club, 15,000
1996	Pierrot, 20,000
1997	Hoppus Poke-us, 10,000
1997	MerBear, Club, 15,000
1997	Peddler, WDW, 5,000
1998	Little Bear Peep, 15,000
1999	Millennium Collection, 2000
1999	Little Miss Muffy, Club
2000	A Spot of Tea, Club

SPECIAL LIMITED EDITIONS

1996	Paint the Town Red, 4,500
1997	Puttering Around, 2,500
1999	Miss Muffy Belle, Event
2000	Muffy Ahead of Her Time, Event

SPECIAL ONE-OF-A-KINDS FOR WDW AUCTIONS

1997	Muffy In WonBearland, $16,000
1998	The Stroke of Midnight, $9,000
1999	Thumbearlina, $9,000

CHRISTMAS ORNAMENTS

1992: Angel / FirTree / Snowbear / Gingerbear
1993: Bal Masqué / Red Flannel / Furrier & Ives / Musical Soiree / Nutcracker / Tree Trimming
1994: Anniversary / Alpine / Snowflake / Muffy of the North
1997: Glass: Muffy of the North / ReinBear / Mouse / Candy C'angel

MUFFY'S SPECIAL FRIENDS

Accessory in Italics

Scottie:	Tree Trimming
Lulu:	Highland Fling: *Bed, Brush, Bowl, Tag & Leash*
	North Pole
	All Paws On Deck
	Sleddin' & Skidaddlin'
	New England
	Spring Bonnets
	Happy Birthday
	Christmas Carol
	Cheerleading
	Salad Ballad
	Square Dancing
	Mercy Me
	Foolish Ghoulish
	Paris Bistro
	Portrait in Black & White
	Sweets for the Sweet
	Blue Pagoda
	Picking Posies
	Grand VanderBall
	Hit The Road
	Adirondack
	Picnic In Provence
	Deck The Halls
	Cirque de la Lune
Catsie:	Wild West
	Undressed
	Bal Masqué
	Alpine
	Flower Festival
	Equestrienne
	Tricky Treat
	Happy Birthday

	Christmas Carol
	Abearcana
	Picnic In Provence
	Cirque de la Lune
Purrlie:	New England, kitten
	Reading: *Basket & Cushion*
	Salad Ballad
	Lemonade Stand
	Foolish Ghoulish
	Portrait in Black & White
	Blue Pagoda
	Grand VanderBall
	Hit The Road
	Adirondack
	Picnic In Provence
	Deck The Halls
	Cirque de la Lune
Patti:	Down On The Farm
	Flower Festival
	Square Dancing
Mary, Webster, Lucy	
	Down On The Farm
	Flower Festival
Rudy:	Down On The Farm
	Flower Festival
	Sweets For The Sweet
Bud & Rose:	Flower Festival
Turkey:	Pilgrim
Seal:	Muffy Of The North
Swan:	Czarina
Penguin:	Polar
Spider:	Little Miss Muffy
Bruce:	Adirondack
Hazel Nutt:	Squir'lfriend

MUFFY'S EXPANDING UNIVERSE
VanderBear merchandise licensed by NABCO

Christopher Radko Ornaments:
1997 Muffy *Sleddin' and Skidaddlin'*
      Muffy *Portrait in Black & White*
1998 Muffy *Plum Fairy*
      Muffy *Candy C'angel*, Roger's Gardens Exclusive
      Muffy *GingerBear*
1999 Muffy *Hearts & Flowers*
      Muffy *Grand VanderBall*
      Muffy *Picking Posies*, Roger's Gardens Exclusive
      Hoppy *Grand VanderBall*
      Hoppy *Messenger of Love*
2000 Muffy *A Christmas Carol*
      Hoppy *A Christmas Carol*
      Czarina *Muffina*
      Muffy *Santa's Workshop*
      Hoppy *Santa's Workshop*
      Muffy *Petite GingerBear*
      Muffy *Petite Portrait in Black and White*

New Muffy Products From Crown Crafts:
Muffy Winter Princess woven throw, limited edition of 2500 packaged in collector's box
Life is One Big Dress-Up woven throw, wall hanging, and 3 conversation pillows

Goodwin Weavers: *Pajama Game* - Throw, Pillows, Bell Pull, and Wall Hanging

Peck Aubrey, Kidoodles "paper dolls" and static vinyl outfits:
Muffy - *Happy Birthday, Rainy Day, Sewing Lesson, Sleddin' & Skidaddlin',* and *Square Dancing*
Hoppy - *Happy Birthday, Rainy Day, Sewing Lesson, Sleddin' & Skidaddlin',* and *Square Dancing*
Lulu - *Happy Birthday, Paris Bistrot, Salad Ballad,* and *Square Dancing*
Oatsie - *Abearicana, Equestrienne,* and *Square Dancing*
Purrlie - *Lemonade* and *Salad Ballad*

Imperial Wall Coverings: Wallpaper Borders in Outdoor Sports and Family Album

Schurman Fine Papers:
Gift Wrap - *Happy Birthday* and *Salad Ballad*
Gift Bags - *Happy Birthday, Salad Ballad,* and *Walking in Eggshells*
Gift Enclosures - *Happy Birthday, Salad Ballad,* and *Muffy Bunny*
Note Cards - *Bear Necessities,* die-cut note card and sticker set
Greeting Cards and Blank Note Cards
Easter Stickers

Chronicle Books:
Address Book
Note Card Set
Blank Journals - Portrait and *Signature*
Calendar 2000
Muffy's Scrapbook

MUFFY IN PRINT
Here are just a few of the places to look for Muffy.

Books
Greene, Joan and Menten,Ted, *The Complete Book of Teddy Bears,* "North American Bear Co.," page 366, Publications International, 1989
Hockenberry, Dee, *The Teddy Bear Companion,* "North American Muffy Bears," page 113, Cowles Magazines, Inc., 1995
Magnolis, Argie, *The Teddy Bear Sourcebook,* "North American Bear Co.," page 179, Betterway Books, 1995
Menton, Ted, *The Joy of Teddy Bears,* "North American Bear Co., pages 80-81, Publications International, LTD, 1991
Michaud, Terry and Doris, *Contemporary Teddy Bear Price Guide,* "North American Bear Company," pages 133-135, Hobby House Press, 1992
Mullins, Linda, *American Teddy Bear Encyclopedia,* "North American Bear Co.," pages 96-99, Hobby House Press, 1995
Mullins, Linda, *4th Teddy Bear & Friends Price Guide,* "North American Bear Co.," pages 5, 20-24, Hobby House Press, 1993
Mullins, Linda, *Teddy Bears Past & Present, Volume II,* "North American Bear Co.," pages 103, Hobby House Press, 1991
Mullins, Linda, *Teddy Bear & Friends Identification & Price Guide,* "North American Bear Co.," page 27, Hobby House Press, 2000
Pearson, Sue and Ayers, Dottie, *Teddy Bears,* "The North American Bear Co.," page 109, Macmillan, 1995
Stanford, Maureen and O'Neill, Amanda, *The Teddy Bear Book,* "Collectable Bears Today," page 136-137, Simon & Schuster, 1994
_____, *Best of Teddy Bear & Friends,* pages 83, 161, 162, Hobby House Press, 1992

Magazines
"Back to School," Cover of *Teddy Bear And Friends,* October 1992
"The Magic of Muffy," *Teddy Bear Review,* May/June 1992
Michaud, Terry and Doris, "That Marvelous Muffy," *Toy Box,* Winter 1992
"Muffy Models Our Tailor Made Togs," Cover *Teddy Bear Review,* January/February 1995
Perry, Candy, "Muffy Mania," *Teddy Bear Times,* January/February 1996
Praytor, Shirley Vaughan, *Teddy Bear And Friends,* "Muffy Moments" feature article, January/February 1995 – December 1999
"The Ultimate Muffy Collector," *Teddy Bear Review,* May/June 1999
"Muffy Makes Merry," *Teddy Bear Review,* November/December 1999

Newspapers
Tousignant, Mary Lou, "Wooing Collectors with Animal Charm and Magnetism," *Washington Post,* September 11, 1995
"Costly Cubs," *Chicago Tribune,* November 14, 1994

North American Bear Company is always willing to answer collector's questions.

Catalogs: Older North American catalogs have become very collectible. There are over 47 catalogs and catalog supplements that include the VanderBears along with other North American Bear products. One unusual catalog is a box of 4 x 6 postcards with index tabs; in the VanderBear category there were 5 cards: the bare VanderBears, Black Velvet Family with Muffy Christening, Cruisewear Family, Taffeta Family, and Muffy Witch. Starting in 1996 the VanderBears had their own catalog. Current and some recent catalogs are available from North American Bear Company. Call for availability and cost.

Missing Pieces: If you are missing a hangtag or a piece from one of your Muffy outfits, North American Bear Company does have some extras available if the outfit is current or recently retired. Hangtags are free but there may be a small charge for other items. Put your request in writing or call for information.

Muffy VanderBear Fan Club: See pages 126 and 127

Tours: North American Bear Co. conducts tours of their Chicago warehouse which includes their Muffy® display. Call their Public Relations Co-Ordinator for information. The Design Studio in New York City is not open to the public.

North American Bear Co., 401 N. Wabash, Suite 500 • Chicago, IL 60611 • (312) 329-0020
North American Bear Co., 4A Scampston Mews • London, England W10 6HX • 01732-36017
Web site: http://www.nabear.com

GLOSSARY

Boxed: For this Guide we have included the box in the description only when the box is illustrated and it adds to the secondary value of the accessory. In other words, plain cardboard or white boxes are not included.

FD / Factory Dressed: A plastic fastener is used to attach accessories to the bear. It is usually used for shoes, hats, or headbows. In this guide we have indicated factory attached items on Muffy only.

Hangtag: Special illustrated tags that come with every dressed bear, every outfit, and some accessories. Most of the hangtags will contain the name of the collection. They are usually hung around the neck of a dressed bear, but sometimes are tied to the wrist. The proper hangtag adds to the value of any retired piece.

Header: An illustrated heavy paper cover that is stapled over the plastic bag of most packaged outfits. If there is a hanger, it pokes through a precut slot in the header. Some headers on accessories have a hole for display hanging. Some of the older outfits that we frequently find without headers are the family Cruisewears. In 1996, some older headers were replaced with new headers that included the Collection name and a bar code, as well as new colors. Headers frequently change during the production of a Collection but the value of the item is not affected.

Limited Edition: There are two types of Limited Edtions; some are limited to time of production and some are limited to a specific number.

MIB: Mint In Box - in perfect new condition with hangtag and original box

MIP: Mint In Package - outfits with headers that are in perfect condition, have never been removed from the package, and with all pieces

OF: Outfit - most outfits came packaged with headers as described above. There is some discrepancy between collectors as to whether all of the older outfits came packaged with headbows. North American Bear Co. thinks that they did, but some collectors feel that they did not.

Retired: For the retired dates we use dates when the item was announced to be retired by NABCO. Sometimes retired items are sold out before their official retirement date and in other cases retired items are still available for dealers to reorder into the next year. Traditionally retirements are announced three times a year, in May, September, and December. Family members of a Collection (Cornelius, Alice, Fluffy, and Fuzzy) are usually retired a few months before Muffy and Hoppy, so different parts of a Collection may have different retirement dates.

2000 Price Guide and Index

It is difficult to print an accurate Price Guide for retired items, because values change so rapidly and vary in different parts of the country. We have included a range of prices based on our contacts during the Summer of 2000. Prices are for **factory dressed bears only** with hangtags and in **mint** condition. Accessory prices listed are also for mint condition with boxes. In the past few years, Internet auction sites have created a convenient place to sell and buy, resulting in lower secondary prices. But serious collectors have found it is better to buy from a reputable dealer and pay a little more, because items listed in auctions are often in poor condition or missing important parts, and many sellers do not offer a return policy if an item is not as described. In the ORP column is the original suggested retail prices at the time of issue. In the 2000 column is the suggested retail price for Summer 2000, or the secondary market value of a retired item at that time. Retired items are indicated with an R.

COLLECTION	PG	Muffy ORP	Muffy 2000	Hoppy ORP	Hoppy 2000	Family ORP	Family 2000	Accessories ORP	Accessories 2000
A BUSHEL OF FUN - APPLE ANTICS	118	35	35	35.50	35.50				
Apple Basket/Apple Cart	118							10/16	10/16
ABEARICANA Oatsie/Chair/Basket	102	38	38	38.50	38.50			34/16/16	34/16/16
AHEAD OF HER TIME - R Watch - **R**	124	40	40-50					10	10-20
A SPOT OF TEA Tea Cup	118	95	95					20	20
ADIRONDACK - ALL SPRUCED UP	111	33	33	33.50	33.50	264	264		
Lulu/Purrlie/Bruce/Sled/Accessories								15/10/30/18/17	15/10/30/32/17
ALL PAWS ON DECK - R Lulu - **R**/ Boat - **R**	76	38.50	40.50	39	41	284	302	15/64	16.50/68
ALPINE - R Oatsie - **R**	53	35	35-50	35.50	35-50	280	280-300	28	30-40
Sleigh-**R** /Tree - **R**								30/47	30-75/47-55
ANGEL - R	28	40	100-200						
ANNIVERSARY - R	66	45	45-75						
Anniversary Pin	70							5	5
ARMOIRE	36							96	108
Armoire Accessories I - **R**	40							35	50-75
Boot Box/Hangers	67							6.50/6.50	7/7
Hat Boxes - **R**/Garment & Shoe Bag	67							14/14	15-20/15
ARTISTES AT WORK Accessories/Cards	119	33	33	33.50	33.50			24/15	24/15
BACK TO SCHOOL - R	32	31	50-100	31.50	45-60				
Desk-**R** /Watch-**R** /Notebook - **R**								22/36/9	50-100/45/18
BALLET RECITAL - R	43	35	50-65	35.50	50-65				
BAL MASQUE - R Oatsie-**R**/Recaimer-**R**	45	37	40-125	37.50	40-100	276	300-400	26/380	40-50/400-500
BARE BEARS: Tush Tag - **R**	99	12	100-200	—	—	102	200-300		
Loop Tag - **R**	99	—	50-100	—	—	—	150-200		
Current Tag		17	20	17.50	20.50	135	165.50		
BATHTIME - R Towels-**R**/Tub-**R**	69	33	35-45	33.50	35-40			7/29	9/50-75
Washstand-**R**/Pitcher - **R**								23/12	30-55/30-60
BEACH - R Chair & Umbrella-**R**	30	24	25-35					16	20-45
BED	36							60	60
Bedding Accessories	41							22	23
BEEKEEPING - R	57	32	35-50	32.50	35-50	247.50	250-350		
Honey Jar Lg.-**R**/Jar Sm. - **R**/Sticker Book-**R**								34/20/4.50	35-50/20-30/5
BLACK CAT Glitter - **R**	20	23	75-125						
BLACK CAT Stitched - **R**			50-75						
BLUE PAGODA: Lulu/Purrlie	103	36	36	36.50	36.50			15/9.50	15/9.50
Tea Set/Linen Set/Gazebo with table								31.50/16/12	31.50/16/12
BOUDOIR - R Vanity-**R**/Screen-**R**/Acc.-**R**	67	35	37.50					50/28/37	55/30/50
BUNNY: Wicker Basket- **R** / Plastic Basket	23	25	40-50/33						
BUTTERFLY - R	46	80	200-400						
CANDY C'ANGEL - R	97	50	50						
CHECKMATES - R Chess Set-**R**/Table Set - **R**	77	33	35	33.50	35.50			60/98	60-75/98-125
CHEERLEADING - R Lulu-**R**/Accessories - **R**	89	38.50	40	39	40.50			18.50/18	18.50/19-25

COLLECTION	PG	Muffy ORP	Muffy 2000	Hoppy ORP	Hoppy 2000	Family ORP	Family 2000	Accessories ORP	Accessories 2000
CHERRY PIE - R Pie Safe-R/Cherry Pie - R	49	35.50	39			C 88	C 101.50	32/5	36/6
CHICK - R	30	27	30-60						
CHRISTENING I - R	11	18	250-500						
CHRISTENING II - R	11		100-200						
CHRISTENING III - R	11		100-200						
CHRISTENING IV	11		29						
CHRISTMAS CAROL - R Lulu- R/ Oatsie- R	91	44	46	44.50	46.50	345	400-500	19/33.50	19/36-50
Muff & Reticule- R/Lantern- R /Landau - R								12/24/112	12/ 25/ 150-200
CIRQUE DE LA LUNE Oatsie/Lulu/Purrlie	120	32	32	32.50	32.50			30/23/14	30/28/14
Tent/Accessories								30/20	30/20
CLASSIC BLACK VELVET - R	10					144	200-300		
CLOTHES RACK	63							15	15
CLUBHOUSE - R Kit-R/Cigar box - R	68	31	34	31.50	34.50	FZ 48	FZ 52	18/20	19/21
CLUB: Kit I - R	126							12	50-100
Scarf/Tote Bag - R	8							8/9.50	8/25-30
Rose Frame/Fan Box	27							11/10	11/10
Soft Cover Album III - R/Photo Album								4.50/15	10/15
Kit II/ Club Stationery & Stickers								22/7.50	22/7.50
MerBear Box/Clock/Furrypouch								12/10/10	12/10/10
Brooch/Sweatshirt/T-shirt								6/25/15	6/25/15
Birthday Cards								6	6
COCOA BUNNY Wheelbarrow	84			38	40			20	21
COLLECTOR EGGS	64							13	6
CRUISEWEAR/tush - R	14	18.50	75-195			162	200-400		
CRUISEWEAR/snap - R			75-150						
CRUISEWEAR/velcro - R			50-125						
CZARINA - R	78	42	42						
DAISY PETALS	121	33	33						
DAY IN THE COUNTRY I - R	17	19.50	125-150			175	200-300		
DAY IN THE COUNTRY II - R			50-100						
DECK THE HALLS WITH BOWS & DOLLIES	122	34	34	34.50	34.50				
Lulu/Purrlie/Tree								20/16/60	20/16/60
DISPLAY: Acrylic Display - R	22								—
Boutique Header - R	23								—
Display Stands: SM/MD/LG	63								2.50/4/7
DOWN ON THE FARM: - R Cart-R	47	34	39					20	30-75
Patti/Mary/Rudy								20 /12/11	21/ 12.50/ 11.50
Webster/Lucy/Display Box								8.50/9/2.50	9/9.50/2.50
DUTCH TREAT - R	48	37	50-75	37.50	50-75				
EASTER FANTASY - R	38	31.50	36-45	32	36-45				
EGG PAINTING - R Paint Set - R/Egg Cups-R	64	32	32-40	32.50	33-40			15/14	15/15-30
EQUESTRIENNE - R Oatsie - R	59	37	40-60	37.50	40-60			29	40-60
FABEARGÉ Eggs	123	32	32	32.50	32.50			22	22
FIGURINES	70							12	6
FIR TREE - R	36	44	150-400						
FLOWER FESTIVAL - R Bud & Rose	56	32.50	50-100	33	50-100			9/9	10/10
Six Friends - R/Garland - R								91.50/9	100-150/15
FOOLISH GHOULISH Lulu/Purrlie/T-shirts	97	35	35	35.50	35.50			17/ 10.50/ 14-30	17/ 10.50/ 14-30
FORTUNE TELLING - R Accessories - R	42	36	41.50	36.50	42			26	30-40

COLLECTION	PG	Muffy		Hoppy		Family		Accessories	
		ORP	2000	ORP	2000	ORP	2000	ORP	2000
FUN & FASHION, KID-SIZED: Muffy Watch								20	20
Muffy Key Chain: Muffy • Hoppy								5/5	5/5
Friends: Backpack Purse • Tote Bag								16/16	16/16
Umbrella • Patches								15/6	15/6
Plush Backpack • Plush Wallet								22/10	22/10
Muffy Plush Scarf: Muffy • Hoppy								10/10	10/10
FURRIER & IVES - R	21	28	150-400			221	300-500		
GALLERY FRAMES	70							18	9
GARDEN PARTY	116	37	37	37.50	37.50	272	272		
Gazebo/Cloth & Cushions/Sandwich Set								20/18/14	20/18/14
GIBEARNY - R Garden Bench - R	31	31	40-100			228	250-300	96	250-350
GIFT-T0-GO	117	65.50	65.50						
GINGERBEAR - R	54	46	100-200						
GRAND TOUR/TRAVEL Diary/Watch	60	37	40					11/42	11.50/46
GRAND VANDERBALL	104	40	40	40.50	40.50	320	320		
Lulu/Purrlie/Gingerbear Box & Dessert Tray								19/10/24	19/10/24
Punch Set/Table & Chair Covers/Tiara								15/23/14	15/23/14
HANGER - Plush - R	18								40-50
HAPPY BIRTHDAY - R Oatsie/Lulu - R	88	38	39	38.50	39.50			32.50/16	35/16.50
Tablecloth Set- R /Party Set - R/Cake - R								17/15/8.50	18/15/10-20
HEARTS & FLOWERS	82	35	37						
HIGHLAND FLING - R Lulu - R/Wreath - R	61	37	40-75	37.50	40-60	290	290-300	10.50/36	11-20/36-40
Stocking - R/Snowdome - R								13/60	13/80-100
HIGH TEA - R Chairs: Small/Large - R	24	28	50-100			198	200-300	18/22	50-100 ea.
HIT THE ROAD Lulu/Purrlie/Backdrop/Gear	112	33	33	33.50	33.50			16/10/22/16	16/10/22/16
HOPPUS POKE - US - R	94			72	72				
JAM SESSION Jars/Cookware/Stove	110	34	34	34.50	34.50			12/16/85	12/16/85
KYOTO BLOSSOM - R	56	35.50	36-60	36	36-50			16	30-50
LEMONADE STAND	96	34	34	34.50	34.50				
Purrlie/Stand/Pitcher & Glasses								9.50/10/19	9.50/10/19
LITTLE BEAR PEEP - R	105	90	90						
LITTLE MISS MUFFY - R	112	75	75-125						
LULU / Bed/ Bowl	60							10.50/5.50/5	11.50/6/5
Brush - R /Tag & Leash								5.50/5	5.50/5
MERCY ME - R	93	37	37	37.50	37.50				
Lulu - R/Bag - R/Ambulance & Stretcher - R								19/19.50/32	19/19.50/32
MESSENGER OF LOVE Scooter	92			39	40			22	22
MERBEAR - R	98	90	125-175						
MILLENNIUM COLLECTION - R	113	250	300-500						
Millennium Porcelain Box								17	17
MISS MUFFY BELLE - R	114	40	40-75						
MOMMY & ME - R Furniture (set of 3) - R	37	31	50-100			A 68	A 75-200	89	150-250
Tea Set - R /Frame - R								20/8	30-50/15
MOUSE - R	79	49.50	75-100						
MOZART - R Spinet - R/Theatre Kit - R	74	39.50	42	40	42.50			60/20	68/21
MUFFY MAIL & PAPER GOODS									
Christmas Cards - R	28							10.50	20-40
Gift Enclosure/Greeting Card	48							.70/1.50	.70/1.50
Holiday: Gift Tags/ Pop-Up Cards/ Stickers	55							4/5/3	4/2.50/3